INTERPERSONAL
COMMUNICATION

COMMUNICATION SCIENCE
AND TECHNOLOGY

*Designed for Communication Leaders in the Media, Libraries
and Information Specialization*

PATRICK R. PENLAND, *Editor*

INTERPERSONAL COMMUNICATION:

COUNSELING, GUIDANCE AND RETRIEVAL FOR MEDIA, LIBRARY AND INFORMATION SPECIALISTS

Patrick R. Penland
UNIVERSITY OF PITTSBURGH
PITTSBURGH, PENNSYLVANIA

Aleyamma Mathai
FAIRLEIGH-DICKINSON UNIVERSITY
RUTHERFORD, NEW JERSEY

MARCEL DEKKER, INC. New York 1974

MARCEL DEKKER, INC.

270 Madison Avenue, New York, New York 10016

LIBRARY OF CONGRESS CATALOG CARD NUMBER: 74-77109

ISBN: 0-8247-6187-1

Current printing (last digit):
10 9 8 7 6 5 4 3 2 1

PRINTED IN THE UNITED STATES OF AMERICA

COMMUNICATION SCIENCE AND TECHNOLOGY

An Introduction to the Series

Since midcentury there has been an exponential increase in the volume of recorded knowledge and a revolution in the control and transfer of information by means of electronic technology. These changes have not only brought the resource specializations of media, library, and information science into a closer working relationship, but have been the impetus for the creation of a new profession, that of resource communicator. Resource sharing and computer networking have made it difficult for these three specializations to hang onto outmoded autonomies. Creative professionals have been released by technology to explore their role as advocates and agents of change in the affairs of human beings. This commonality of concern for people, as distinct from the production, control, and transfer of materials, is slowly being articulated by leaders in the three specializations.

The common profession of communicator, whose objective is to develop communication services based on a network of all-encompassing resource infrastructures, has emerged from the specializations of media, library, and information science. In practice, of course, some variations may still exist in the services provided. With this series these variations need no longer receive greater attention than the needs of the whole human being seeking help for his own behavioral self-control and self-design. As a result, the client need no longer be shunted around from media center to library and adult-education agency or to information center regardless of the fact that it is the surprise value of knowledge within a behavioral context which he needs and not necessarily the documents and resources guarded by each type of resource agency.

The general purpose of publications in the Communication Science and Technology series is to integrate professional and historical developments, as so many other texts in the field do not. These publications feature a service-oriented and conceptually-interlocking system of communication principles and communication services based within the traditions and practice of media, libraries, and information science. Pub-

934390

EDUCATION

lications in the series provide the basis for a bold new approach for the
resource communicator, one which emphasizes communication over
agency standards, deals directly with the problems of living rather than
with documentation, and meets controversy when and where it arises in
the neighborhood without traveling to the media, library, or information
center.

The disciplines that create new knowledge will be interested in this
approach to the development of communications. The profession of resource communicator holds considerable promise as a significant social
method for more rapidly closing the gap between research findings and
their application to the affairs of the common man. In addition, the series
will be of singular importance to any profession which employs the resources of recorded knowledge to solve human problems or develops
guidelines for planned social change, such as is done in education, communications, and politics. A case in point is adult education, the principles and methods of which have long served as a source of inspiration
and guidance to librarians. These professions can view the emergence
of resource communicators not as an encroachment upon their affairs
but as an opportunity for enhanced partnership in serving public needs.

These publications can be employed as guides for practice, in-service training, and the continuing education of resource-center staff.
The theoretical foundations of behavioral psychology, group-systems
analysis, and community sociodrama will be of particular significance
to the busy supervisor called upon to provide a rationale for communication
services in media, libraries, and information centers. Within this
framework the methods and techniques are developed for creating, chan-
neling, and applying information surprise to the concerns and interests
of the patron whether as an individual, a small group, or the neighborhood and community enterprise.

These publications will help the profession to create the conditions
within which communicative activity can occur. Through communication,
it will enhance its image as a socially accountable profession which can
handle socially unstable subsystems. More specifically, the reader, be
he general or professional, will find answers to questions such as the
following.

What social purposes, function, and even, procedures
do the resource professions share with each other and
with other professions in society?

For what social change among which publics are the
resource professions responsible? Within what contexts can the change process be carried out by resource communicators?

What means can be employed to accomplish planned
social change? What factors can be exploited in order
to motivate citizens to participate and to communicate?

How can the infrastructure of resources be deployed in
order to support a communications profession? How can
the gap between indexed message space and the nonverbal
and audio-visual message space of the people be closed?

The volumes in the series may be used as textbooks, supplementary
readings, or as background reading for the informed citizen, especially
the wide range of persons who use media, libraries, and information
centers as well as those who serve as trustees or board members of institutions which maintain resource centers. The volumes in the series
cover concepts and describe methods that would be useful in particular
for

Audiovisual and media specialists in a wide range of
centers serving patrons with various socioeconomic,
cultural, and educational levels

Librarians in all types of agencies and who provide
services to patrons of varying age levels, education,
and socioeconomic status

Information specialists, including systems analysts and
designers, at various levels of service

The broad range of adult education facilities administered by
a variety of institutions and agencies as well as educators
at all levels and, in particular, media and library and information science faculties

Sociologists, political scientists and politicians, urban-
ologists and urban information systems specialists

Community planners (urban planners), public admin-
istrators, community leaders (lay and professional),
communication specialists (all levels)

> Professional staff and lay volunteers of the numerous
> information hot lines and neighborhood information
> centers

The models presented and the methods discussed are fundamental
to human affective and cognitive development as it is achieved through
communicative processes. The professional concerned about his own
self-development may wish to peruse these publications for insight into
what is known about human intellectual growth and development. As a
result he may be able to remain in control of his own growth, independent
of outside influences. On the other hand, in those instances when he
finds it useful to seek help from other communicators, the professional
role will become more meaningful and productive for him.

Since the meaning of communication is not self-evident, the resource
professions need a definition and explication of a communicative profession and the relation of applications to the contexts of dyad, group,
and community. With a formulated behavior theory integrated with the
principles of media, library and information science it should be possible
to increase the scope of communication within the mainstream of social-
science research. While many of the examples are taken from "adult"
education as well as the resource specializations, other communicators
will find the approach particularly appropriate to a wide range of human
development professions.

Communications specialists will look to this approach in order to
conceive of their professional difficulties in communication terms and
realize that encounter negotiation and information surprise are the fundamental components of relevance. In general, the many exercises and
simulations are designed to be readily understood by and acceptable to
staff members, while at the same time avoiding the limitation of single
examples without a conceptual framework. The professional methods
of human communication are presented within the psychology of the behavioral cycle. Human-relations training, group dynamics, and decision
making are immersed in small-group sociology. Community psychology
and coordination support the professional methods of persuasion, mass
communication, advocacy, and community development.

PREFACE

When the services of resource agencies are examined with the aid of communication models (their set of principles and methods), one of the weakest areas of professional preparation, inservice training, and development is that of interpersonal communication. Each year many professionally trained recruits enter the field of media, library, and information service with only the most rudimentary human relations training for, and only the slightest awareness of, counseling, interviewing, and guidance. This is compounded by the fact that professional education for client services, historically, has given little formal attention to interpersonal communication and the ability to use it for the broad purposes of the many patrons who use the various resource centers.

There exists in most resource centers today, client services where neither the supervisor nor any of the professional staff have received formal training in communication. While general courses in materials guidance and the problems of viewing, listening and reading have been taught in many professional schools for years, the actual interpersonal methods of communication have been largely obtained by professional personnel through an intuitive understanding of their role on the job. Consequently, professionals who work in client services do not generally serve the patron as catalyst in order to promote patron-conversation and patron-verbalization upon perceptions, nor muster liason with a wide range of community information resources.

This publication lays the basis for training in interpersonal communications which resource specialists need in order to overcome insecurity, lack of ability and the constant inclination to "short-change" the patron in his desire to symbolize and express interests and concerns. The text of this volume in interpersonal communication is written from the viewpoint of resource specialists; and the relationship has been explicated which exists between interpersonal communication, group dynamics and community development psychology. The following points may serve as selected examples of the many values to be found in the text:

Understand the relationship of counseling and advisory work to materials production and information retrieval as well as to develop flexibility in moving from one frame of reference to another with the same patron.

Determine the role and psychological timeliness of materials
in the advisory situation as well as the value of an expanded
range of media materials, community resources and referral
sources.

Identify the methods for guiding the healthy individual towards
a self-actualizing development organized around life stages,
social roles and various coping behaviors for which the guidance process of symbolizing experience and media therapy are
integral elements.

Develop an appreciation of group counseling, and of the relationship of these principles to group behavior, leadership
and the community development enterprise.

Apply relevant findings from the fields of psychology, learning
and communication in order to strengthen the role of the resource
specialist as a change agent.

The citizen concerned over the social relevance of information agencies in his community will find that the present work and others in the
series lay a foundation for the review and coordination of community
information and referral resources. This work and its companion volumes provide a background for the training of those citizen leaders
who volunteer their services in the many information and crises intervention centers so typical of contemporary community life. In this regard, the resource specialist and particularly staff supervisors will
find useful the variety of ideas and situations designed to address the
functions of change agent and information advocate.

The informed citizen will also find in this approach to communication
a powerful tool for his own behavioral development and self-design.
Since most of his real life experiences occur within the interpersonal
environment, information retrieved and presented within this context
will be valuable in a kinetic and practical manner. The objective of
improved professional service is to assist the citizen in all walks of
life to undertake his information and continuing learning projects and
facilitate their completion to his satisfaction.

In general, the purpose of Interpersonal Communication is to extend
present practice to include research findings in counseling, guidance
and interviewing, as well as place these newer modes of communication
within the framework of principles and significant applications in the

media, library and information profession. The book also deals with
models of human effectiveness in the use of information surprise which
are intended to help the resource specialists conceptualize the upper
limits of human information processing. By considering these practical
models of information processing, the reader may be better able to syn-
thesize his own approach to human communication.

An orientation to communication's theory, as well as learning and
counseling theory, provides a base for this endeavor. The publication
presents a synthesis of the structure and organization of the variant and
often discrete services to individual patrons of media, library and information center, such as counseling, guidance, interviewing, audiovisual therapy, tutorials and "surpriseful" information retrieval. It
is based on the philosophy that the ultimate goal of services to the individual is to maximize human effectiveness through the developing
ability to exploit information resources.

This book will be of value to media, library and information specialists in a wide range of settings who are responsible for the continuing
education of all citizens. The work is primarily behavioral in orientation
and draws widely from other disciplines, particularly psychology and
sociology. Professional staff whether their roles be media therapists,
advisory counselors, bibliotherapists, reference retrievers or information
scientists will find the book useful in conceptualizing the process of
human development and in formulating their roles in facilitating such
development.

Hopefully, this work will stimulate overdue innovation within the
resource specializations by helping communicators grow in personal
and professional effectiveness. Since human development is a lifelong
and lifewide task, this material may be useful to the professional resource
specialist in settings ranging from children's services to work with the
aged. Several aspects set this book apart from other works in the field.
It presents a coherent description of the processes of the human behavioral
cycle organized around the transactional nature of the citizen's environment and elaborated in terms of developmental tasks, coping behaviors
and professional change-agent roles.

This publication is also unique in the attention it gives to the resource
specialist in media, library and information science as a behavioral
scientist and as an agent for change. The communicator is viewed as
an advocate for continuing education. A communications specialist can
facilitate the development of patrons through interpersonal and group

negotiations, and also can act as an innovator for constructive change
processes in neighborhood, organizational and cultural milieu within
which his patrons develop. The work is geared to the needs of the communicator attempting to work with a full range of socioeconomic and cultural differences. While primary attention is directed to the function of
a resource communicator in behavior modification, the logical retrieval
of data is not neglected for its supportive role in the human interface.

The emphasis today has shifted from retrieval skills alone to include
relationships in which the surprise value of information is pursued through
the behavioral cycle of stimulus, interpretation and response. Hopefully
the day is past when the resource specialist can remain objectively aloof
from human change. This work lays a basis for such a critical reorientation
of the resource specializations of media, library and information science.
With training, the helping interface can be entered into not simply as a
method for transfering data from organized and indexed message space
but as the means by which professional staff can engender the meaning
of surpriseful information within other human beings.

CONTENTS

INTERPERSONAL
COMMUNICATION

ONE

INTRODUCTION

Interpersonal communication is an integral element of the profession and the essential method for assisting human development in the context of a dyad relationship between the patron and communicator in the media, library, and information specializations. It assumes a helping relationship on the part of the communicator which is dedicated to individual freedom and self-actualization. Various aspects of this helping relationship have been known as audiovisual therapy, counseling and advisory, as well as tutorials in the strategies of information search and retrieval.

Developmental counseling and audiovisual therapy are needed when the patron has not, or cannot organize his unresolved personal experiences nor has developed symbols with which to discuss "felt" needs. With counseling, an understanding about his life experiences develops as well as eventual cognitive flexibility. Then, and only then, does the patron have the mental concepts under such personal control as will make it possible to employ relevant retrieval strategies. The communicator takes the patron where he is, helps him conceptualize "felt" needs as well as identify and employ appropriate problem solving techniques.

In interpersonal communication, each patron is considered to be a responsible participant in his own growth processes and not merely a passive receiver of the communicator's advice, information, or instructional program. The communicator begins with the person where he is and endeavors to understand him as a whole person (16). Each patron's progress in affective and cognitive development effects and is effected by his personal, real life situations. Such patron-oriented concerns as these are the only "items on the agenda" of interpersonal communication between a patron and the professional change agent.

The professional communicator may well be acquainted with the producation and contents of all types of materials as well as the scope of community resources but his essential function is to help the patron focus on his concerns rather than on the communicator's personal and professional enthusiasms. Communicators are skilled in such self-control and do not as Flexner says, "...let personal enthusiasm for books and

1

a desire for perfection influence the selection of titles for lists to such
an extent that they meet the librarian's ideal rather than the reader's
needs (40)." Once the patron has been helped to symbolize a previously
"felt" need, the counselor encourages him to develop a plan for problem
solving which may include community resources far more particularized
than the media center can handle.

The generalized problem solving model has been defined for librarians
by Booton as a program involving "self education through books and other
resources of the library and community (18)." Since self education is
continuous, the patron looks to the resource agency as a method with
which he can interact whenever motivated. He expects some knowledge
of his behavior within the system and some help in estimating the relevance of retrieved information on his life style. Gagne (42) has described the method succinctly:

> The system assumes a knowledge of the basic skills, but
> it does have remedial loops for those needing extra help
> with the problems being as much as possible related to
> real life.

> The system must have some means of external organization
> of information to promote retention of material learned.

> Following learning, there must be productive thinking;
> otherwise, the system would be of no value.

COUNSELING AS AN IMPERATIVE

Counseling, as one of the methods employed by the resource change
agent in a dyadic context, may be nonverbal or oral. Nonverbal counseling employs media in a therapeutic way. The patron is encouraged
to compose messages in audiovisual materials. The design is composed
by a process of intuitive discovery as the patron works out a felt need
in audiovisual materials. Once the message (film, tape, artifact) is
completed, the patron can expose (show, send) it to the professional
change agent who, in turn, endeavors to get the patron to talk about his
perceptions of the creation.

Aided by the techniques of oral counseling, the patron's perception
of his felt need moves from a generally diffused state (confusion) into
differentiation. The patron is encouraged to talk about his felt need by
describing experiences associated with it. Articulation helps the patron

to integrate his thoughts and eventually compress the meandering threads
into a concept set. In driving towards symbolization, towards which
he has been motivated by the professional change agent and his own goals,
the patron is able to produce a verbal abstract of his experiences. In
the process, he has grown confident that this expressed statement is
congruent with felt needs.

The patron's expressed statement can now be considered by the professional change agent in terms of particular resources and their use.
Rather than telling the patron what to do, the advisor suggests some
patterns of intrapersonal communication based in viewing, listening and
reading materials. The developmental task implications which have
been expressed in the patron's statement are sought by the patron and
change agent working together in as wide a range of media materials
as possible. As soon as the developmental values are located in materials, that document subset is arranged into a "ladder" of intrapersonal
communication. The patron is encouraged to peruse this lattice of in-
tersecting surpriseful experiences.

Actually, the patron should already be deeply motivated to participate
in the lattice of communicative activity developed with the help of the
professional change agent because the drive towards symbolization is
strong in the human adaptive control organism. There are few if any
healthy human beings who are not strongly motivated to relate the often
disparate accumulations of daily experience to organized message space.
The nonverbal and audiovisual message space of the people is not suf-
ficiently "abstract" to guide the behavioral vector so necessary to the
self-directing individual.

A plateau may be reached in the developmental cycle when the patron
needs to be challenged again by additional surpriseful information. If
he returns to a media, library or information resource center, the professional change agent will assist him in developing appropriate reference and retrieval strategies. The actual tactics are negotiable depending
upon the patron's entry point and upon his perception of where he wants
to be taken through organized message space. In many instances, however, the patron will need some tutorial and instructional assistance
not only in resource organization but also in reference and retrieval
patterns: typed lookup questions, stochastic document browsing, co
ordinated correlation of regressive index terms.

Counseling and media advisory service constitute the general
method by which the change agent helps the patron predispose himself

to reference retrieval and instruction. Once a readiness to learn has
been developed, the patron can progress to and participate more effectively in experiences designed for communicative activity. These activities may be individually self-directed; or they may be group self-directed in those instances where socialization and group determination
are necessary. In any event, planning and development is largely the
responsibility of the patron and may sometimes be undertaken in conjunction with the professional catalyst.

The general problem solving model comprises the method employed
by the patron in this developmental process. The model itself is broadly
inclusive of almost an infinite number of variations and combinations.
The resource change agent in the media, library, and information center
employs the model as a method for encouraging the patron to use the
knowledge and competencies which the agency has to diffuse. These
learnings or outcomes are unique to the profession and imply a contract
which the patron has come to the resource center to claim.

Functionally, Maxfield (91) identified five levels in interpersonal
communication whether it is used for therapeutic, communicative, or
educational purposes. The first two levels of counseling include clinical counseling and psychiatric consultation. Clinical and psychiatric
counseling are conducted by specialists with appropriate graduate
training and clinical experience. These therapists handle referrals
made to them by the professional change agent operating as a third level
collaborator. Parenthetically, clinical and psychiatric counselors may
employ media and library specialists as assistants in order to provide
each patient with interesting activity to occupy his time. These service-
oriented materials specialists sometimes called "bibliotherapists" work
on a team including play, occupational, physical and other adjunctive
therapists supervised by a clinical or psychiatric counselor (143).

Interpersonal communication is a psychological operation, or patron-
communicator interface which may occur at any one or more of these
levels but which involves professional communication only at the three
upper professional levels. Parenthetically, it should be noted that the
difference between lower and upper levels of professional activity should
not be construed as a hierarchial order. The distinctions are rather
to be considered on a spectrum ranging from the most concrete human
experience to the most symbolic and abstract. Therapeutic and psychiatric counseling may appear at one end of the scale while information retrieval would range to the more abstract end of the spectrum.

Counseling properly so-called begins at the third level of competence. Professional counseling is more than advice-giving, although advice and information as well as problem solving may be incorporated into the counseling process. Counseling concerns itself primarily with the identification and extrication of perceptions and attitudes which tend to block thinking and learning. Seeking to bolster the patron's motivation, successful persuasion leads to changes within the patron that will help him develop cognitive flexibility, solve immediate personal problems and make wiser decisions in the future (103).

In the fourth phase of interpersonal communication, advisement occurs as in the case when a materials adviser (so-called reader's adviser) or reference specialist recommends some reading program or an appropriate bibliographic and search technique. Hutchins (64) and later Shores (130) described this function as subject reference work and formulated heuristic techniques under the general problem solving model. More recent writers such as Monroe (99), following Rothstein (121) prefer to compartmentalize this function into three service techniques: information, instruction and guidance. This approach, however, neglects the fact of significant differences which exist between instruction and communication (151).

The fifth level involves the answering of questions as in reference work or in data retrieval. At this level, retrieval is in part a quantitative transfer process once suitable heuristic competencies are employed. The skills involved have been largely reduced to formalize patterns of retrieval (78) and the questions themselves categorized (130) for increased associative power. But of more significance is the fact that the heuristics of information retrieval, if understood and apprehended by the patron, can enhance his own critical and creative thinking in problem solving contexts.

Counseling and resource advisory services have grown as the media, library, and information profession has become more sophisticated in its awareness of interpersonal communication. The interface between change agent and patron is based upon a self-disciplined stance on the part of the resource specialist. Eschewing a conversational mode, the counselor holds verbal communication to a minimum so that he can listen to the patron and think about unspoken needs. Content analysis principles and methods have been used to improve counseling methods and interviewing techniques.

Employing content analysis techniques, the counselor listens to
meaning as it develops out of the interview. The media specialist hypothesizes about the patron's intentions, especially the motivational direction
of unspoken needs, and investigates the experiences which appear to require organization around relevant symbols. The interview is a transactional interface which helps the patron develop some cognitive direction
in his everyday life experiences. Once symbolization, that is cognitive
structure, occurs, then meaningful contact can be made with the corpus
of knowledge as it exists in the resources of message space (104).

Developmental counseling is most often used by the professional
change agent with "healthy" patrons; whereas clients with repressions
or psychoses are referred to clinical or therapeutic counselors. Diag-
nosis in developmental counseling consists of a succession of hypotheses
as to what is occurring in the patron's affective and cognitive domains
(106). The counselor change agent makes inferences about these changes
in the patron in an effort to make his own responses more relevant to
the patron's ill-formed expressions of need and interest.

BEHAVIOR SELF-DESIGN AND SELF-CONTROL

The communicator is an important source of influence on the behavior
of patrons who seek his assistance. Perhaps the most significant aspect
of interpersonal influence is whether the relationship imposes domination
and control on the patron or emancipates him from external control by
increasing his ability to cope with the message space acquired, organized
and indexed by specialists in media, library, and information science.

The ombudsman communicator accepts people where they are in
socially conditioned message space (104). Indexes are maintained and
access to community resources is provided in order to serve as a reality
base for citizen decision making once his mind has been so enlivened
by verbal message space that he can offer socially constructive criticism.

The importance of self-control and self-design to our society is enhanced by the increasing trends in technology and automation. The imperative upon the individual is increasing to build behavioral bridges between humanistic values and the methods and accomplishments of technology. The filling of such a gap is one of the major social purposes of
the resource communicator in media, library, and information agencies.
Behavioral technologists must be exposed to opportunities for humanistic
studies and exploration; while humanists need a more profound understanding of the values and goals of technology.

The concept of self-control along with the associated ideas of freedom and self-improvement are fundamental to the patron-communicator
relationship in the resource specialization of media, library, and information science. A self-actualizing patron is one who directs his own
actions and is master of his environment. He becomes increasingly competent in his ability to guide the transactional nature of his immediate
affairs. The life style of the individual may be unique, but each patron
combines within himeslf certain reactions to features of the environment,
whether sociocultural or physical.

Self-development is integrally related to those environmental considerations which take on a demand character for each individual and
over which he hopes to exert increasing self-control. The function of
the communicator is to help the patron manipulate the "technology" of
behavioral control to his own advantage. Through counseling, guidance,
and problem solving experiences the patron can become proficient in the
procedures necessary to manage and direct his own internal and external actions.

The acquisition of these self-control skills is dependent on the patron's
ability to identify patterns and causes in the behavior to be regulated.
Most people cherish independence and the competence to alter factors
which influence desired changes in behavior. The individual in observing
events around him remembers and analyzes the phenomena which affect
him. By watching the activity of others, he learns to use certain techniques in order to change specific factors in his environment. Intrapersonally he examines his own thought patterns and other nonverbal
data about himself to appraise his own adaptive behavior.

When the patron approaches the media communicator, he suffers
from a tensional state which pressures him to find an answer or solution
to his visceral or informational need. The communicator is empathetic
to the need of the patron and determines the search and retrieval strategy
appropriate to begin satisfying the identified need. Direct interaction
with sources may lead to further modification of the patron's needs as
will further and continual consultation with the media specialist. The
patron may solve his need through exposure to the media itself, the
media librarian or a combination of the two. The tension of the patron
begins to subside when he encounters some information which has some
surprise value. The librarian operates on two levels of interpersonal
encounter: one to solve the immediate congruent need of the patron for
information, and the larger goal to develop a total personality as outlined
in the communicative aims of his agency as well as the communications
profession as a whole.

In the context of nondirective counseling, the communicator helps
the patron to consider the everyday situation within which his concern
or interest emerged. In addition, the immediate antecedents and possible
consequences of such concerns and interests are examined in order to
identify whatever constraints and opportunities may be evident. The
communicator, by means of his interface strategies, endeavors to help
the patron maximize at least the following factors in his own self-actualization:

> Articulation and description of a behavior until patterns
> emerge.
>
> Analysis of antecedent cues and environmental consequences.
>
> Identification of opportunity sets and the surprise value of
> information.
>
> Alteration of antecedents and consequences in problem solving
> and feedback formats.

Self-observation is the first tactic of the patron. This implies that
the patron can attend to his own actions and articulate their occurrence
in order, eventually, to check upon and evaluate his own progress. The
individual who observes his own behavior not only becomes more aware
of himself but also lays the basis for immediate and cumulative feedback on what he does or does not do. The very fact of self-observation
may be reason enough for the individual to feel more positive about himself and subsequently, hopefully, appreciate the role of a resource communicator in the affairs of men.

Environmental surveillance can be considered the second self-control tactic of the individual. This involves analyzing the cues preceding
a behavioral concern or interest and the immediate consequence of it if
any. In the analysis, the patron is led to identify his own likes and dislikes and whether these have had a limiting influence in his specification
of concerns and interests. The patron may consider some evaluation at
this point in the sense of deciding whether he wants to be open or closed
to his environment with all of its liabilities and opportunities.

As a third tactic, the individual can capitalize upon his preferences
and motives by analyzing possible opportunities and identifying those
which are immediately available to him. The patron could rely upon
those opportunities which can be identified by his immediate acquaintances.

The self-actualizing young adult of today does not limit himself to customary boundaries and is always reaching out to find new chances to take. Consequently, wide data access and retrieval is especially important for a range of informationally surpriseful experiences. Patrons resent being limited to the disparate vested interests in resource collections of fragmented media, library, and information centers.

Finally, behavioral programming may be considered the fourth self-control tactic of altering antecedents and consequences in problem solving and feedback contexts. This involves the trial and error process, either mentally or physically, of manipulating behavioral cues and consequences. Environmental planning may also involve eliminating or avoiding situations and conceptual maps in which particular choices are necessary. On the other hand, the tactic may include the rearrangement and manipulation of behavioral antecedents and effects. However, the emphasis is usually upon behavioral modification through such self-administered therapeutic techniques as satisfaction or dissatisfaction over internal and external change.

The self-control process is initiated within a patron by his interaction with some environmental phenomena. His patterns of behavior are unique orchestrations of specific concepts, skills, verbalisms, values and preferences with which he interacts with specific referents in the environment. Some stimuli impinging on his awareness have caused him to pay attention to them. The demand value of the stimuli have aroused his curiosity or resentment.

The patron should be encouraged to articulate and describe his own concerns and interests; otherwise the librarian, if he is not careful, soon finds himself functioning as an advisor or tutor or, in some cases, even as a teacher. In place of inducing patrons to handle their own perceptions, the "teacher" in this case substitutes his own verbal description and analysis of the situation and then assumes that the patron should be able to conceptualize on the basis of this description alone.

The skillful communicator, however, is not caught in this perceptual short circuit. Instead of becoming the active party in the negotiation, he maneuvers the patron into a materials ladder approach designed to be as closely isomorphic as possible to the developmental values being sought by the patron. A film, a videotape or a novel serves as the vicarious version of the patron's developmental tasks and under perusal by the patron, becomes the active component in providing descriptions for the patron's perceptions.

Involvement of the patron at this level of development may take place over some period of time in the experiential history of any individual. The development of many patrons along the continuum of "reading" motivations (125) seems to become arrested at this level and such patrons become fixed in activating recall and conception. In fact the typical patron, out of habit, becomes mesmerized with the plethora of materials available for vicarious experience. Indeed, it is strange that the scope and significance of this problem has received little if any serious investigation, even though in the professional life of any communicator it appears that the majority of his patrons never move beyond this stage of viewing, listening and reading.

For the citizen who is motivated and demands service, the resource component of media, library, and information science is available for tutorials and instruction in library use (109). Here again the communicator is adept in motivating the patron to do his own search in the retrieval from message space and stands ready to assist in a catalytic way. But the formulation and statement of judgements about his case, such as his preferences among the perceived elements and opportunities involved and available to him, become meaningful and liberating when the patron does it for himself by grounding his perception and descriptions in message space. Classified message space becomes the active component in the patron's life to bring some order out of his otherwise disparate human experience.

The objectives of instruction in the use of information, library, and media centers can be extrapolated from the objectives of the profession: promote the maturity of individuals, groups, and communities. Maturity is engendered when the patron is assisted not only to retrieve data from message space but also to negotiate the surprise value obtained from that data and continue to participate in a continuing plan for problem solving his way through life. Problem solving requires an experimental approach, a cognitive flexibility and a motivational pattern to be widely and wisely informed on the part of the citizen.

QUESTION ANALYSIS AND DISCUSSION

The questions which appear below are designed to help the reader determine how the models of individual development and interpersonal communication can be applied to the services which individual patrons expect. The questions may also serve as hypotheses to be tested by the resource specialist in media, library, and information centers as they work to meet human needs.

Guide questions such as these can be kept in mind while reading the text, or considered as points for reflection after an initial reading. No one question is necessarily "keyed" to any single chapter or even a particular section of it. In general, the questions may be answered to the reader's satisfaction only after the reading, reflection and analysis of the entire work.

What is the communicator's orientation to the individual patron? Are the needs and values, for which information is sought, determined by the patron and dependent upon his initiative? If so, is the resource specialist a passive listener?

Is interviewing considered to be a helping relationship in which the patron identifies his own concerns? How does interviewing fit into the general method for helping the patron solve his problem or meet his need?

How are advisory counseling, reference retrieval and tutorials used as alternative (or in combination) methods for the patron to consider?

How does developmental counseling relate to therapy (whether bibliotherapy, or audiovisual materials therapy, or browsing therapy)?

At what point in the behavioral cycle of the patron are the helping relationships of counseling, guidance and retrieval called for, and why?

Why, how and when does the communicator make referral to resources outside the agency? Does the resource specialist have an advocacy role to play in this matter?

What principles and methods in interpersonal relations can be employed by supervisors to evaluate staff performance and promote effective communication within the agency and with the general public who use the resource center?

These questions relate to counseling, guidance and retrieval which constitutes only one context within which the professional change agent operates. In practice, he may specialize in this area but the professional communicator must also be more familiar with and indeed have expertise in the group and community contexts. The human being with whom he

is working is an integrated whole who has to transact his interpersonal
business in any and all contexts. In order to provide help for real life
concerns and interests, the professional change agent must have training
and experience in interpersonal communication and community psychology.

    It may be simple enough to answer a list of questions relating to
interpersonal relations validated on the basis of communication and
learning theory (83). But the communications leader has to keep in mind
the relation of interpersonal communication to group experiences and
the community development enterprise. The set of tasks confronting
the communications change agent in other contexts is taken up and explicated in the other volumes of the series, "Communication Science
and Technology for Communication Leaders in Media, Library, and Information Science." Of particular interest in this regard, Communication
Science and Technology (104), Group Dynamics and Individual Development (108), and Community Psychology and Coordination (105) will be
found immediately useful.

TWO

DEVELOPMENTAL COUNSELING

To many a practicing resource specialist in media, library, and information centers, it may seem pedantic to stress the components of the behavioral cycle. But the only way to know and understand the patron is through the conversational mode in what is known as the developmental interview. The behavioral cycle provides a human and functional guide to the conversation between patron and professional. Without some model or guide, the conversation will scarcely lead anywhere except possibly to pass the time. Even worse as so often happens in traditional librarianship, the readers advisor fills the ear of patrons with all the tidbits of the "wonderful" books he has read.

The patron deserves to be able to participate in a professional conversation that is productive from his point of view. A developmental interface represents both a verbal and a nonverbal interaction between the patron and professional working toward a common goal (118). Interpersonal communication is a give and take process. During the interview, for example, the communicator must encourage the patron to talk, establish a sound relationship of frankness and confidence, link the topic of inquiry to the interest of the patron, focus the patron's attention on the issues in question, and make sure the patron understands what is said (132).

Interpersonal communication is pervasive, and fundamental to all human activity. It is essential to primary group experience, such as the family and reference groups, and constitutes the bulk of important communications on the community level. Of the various levels of communication, interpersonal communication is the least dependent upon writing and other technologies of communication. The application of extensive technology would seriously disrupt its purpose and function. The function of interpersonal communication is to integrate the human organism, intrapersonally and interpersonally. Technology on the other hand functions to send messages through time and space.

Intrapersonal communication is based within an individual human organism. The human organism is a communication system unto itself

and does not require a speaker, message, or a listener in the sense
these terms are used in formal communication. However, reading,
viewing, and listening are essential skills of intrapersonal communication
and integral to the nature of the dialog which takes place within the individual. But, as the human organism moves from intrapersonal to
interpersonal communication, the attempt is made to increase the number and consistency of meanings which occur to it about emerging needs
and drives, as well as the demands of the physical and social setting.

Counseling is a professional form of interpersonal communication
whose purpose is to assist the individual human organism to organize
unresolved experience and develop symbols with which eventually to interrogate the knowledge store, indexed as it is by the professional subject analyst, and possibly to prepare more or less formal communication
messages of his own. Since counseling communication is a complex and
constantly evolving process, audio and video tapings are used to study
and refine the counselor-patron relationship (110).

The dynamics of interviewing is a form of content analysis and consists of a succession of hypotheses as to what is taking place in the cognitive or affective domains of the patron. As nonverbal and verbal
changes appear to occur in the patron, inferences are made by the counselor in an effort to make his own response more pertinent and significant
to the illformed expressions by the patron of his need and interest.
In Table 1 there are a number of questions which may prove useful to
the resource specialist in defining his role in interpersonal communication.

The main characteristics of the counseling relationship include nonverbal, oral and verbal communication. The counseling interview differs from ordinary conversation because one person, the counselor,
remains professionally objective and circumspect in the amount and nature
of his talk. The patron, on the other hand, may say anything which comes
to mind since it is his purpose and sense of direction, or lack of them,
which constitute a counseling interview. While the patron assumes an
active communicative role, the counselor concentrates on the messages
in order to help the patron analyze and interpret his own "conversation."

The purpose served by the counselor is not simply that of a sounding
board. He must listen carefully and develop hypotheses about the patron's
poorly articulated purposes, needs and interests. These hypotheses are
expressed in the form of statements or questions by the counselor and
are under continual modification with feedback from the patron.

Table 1

Professional Communication

Model Components	Feedback
WHO	Who am I in this communication situation? Am I known as a professional change agent? Does the patron have a preconceived view of me? Do I have the training to counsel and guide?
SAYS WHAT	Exactly what is it that I should ask or say in this particular communication situation? Are my purposes clear, well defined and limited? On what key strategies and tactics should my professional help rest?
IN WHAT CHANNEL, THROUGH WHAT MEDIUM	Among the media and methods at hand, which is the most appropriate for this communication job? Is some combination of media and methods desirable?
TO WHOM	Who is this patron? In what context does he live? What expectations does he have of professional help? How can I promote effective two-way communication with this one individual?
WITH WHAT INTENDED EFFECT	What do I want to achieve as a result of this interface? Do I want to change behavior? If so, why should this patron be interested, and what should he be expected to do?

Depending on his theoretical orientation, the therapist in-
tervenes for a variety of reasons. He may wish to help
the patient talk more, become less anxious, obtain insight,
become more aware, or change his outlook and behavior.
His decision to speak or to remain silent reflects what he
believes will contribute to the therapeutic progress. A
therapist's replies may be analyzed in terms of the extent
of his activity, the focus and form of his response, the ambiguity or specificity of his response, the leading or following quality of his response, and the depth of his interpretation (129).

Counseling communication is designed to help the patron identify
and understand his objectives and needs which are yet but dimly perceived and remain scarcely anything more than vague feelings in the
affective domain. As a result of the hypotheses and analyses contin-
ously being made by the counselor, the patron is encouraged to translate
unorganized experience into symbols which thus become accessible to
rational analysis and discourse. At this point, the counselor, acting
as an information negotiator, can assist the patron to interrogate the
indexing file prepared by the information scientist. Simple verbalization,
for its own sake on the part of the counselor, is not enough but must be
accompanied by an appreciation of the significance of what is being expressed by the patron.

INTERACTIVE LISTENING

The counselor, in following the patron's remarks, must attend to
some facets of the discourse and neglect others. He must decide to be
silent or to speak, clarify, question or interpret the comments. He
must organize and interpret what he hears before leading statements
are made. In a sense, all responses to statements by others are interpretations based upon a number of finer distinctions or categories. At
one time, a simple unidimensional approach was taken to the construction
of counseling analysis categories. However, today, counseling interview
analysis has been largely superseded by a multidimensional system.

Obviously, context analysis is at work in the counseling relationship, and because of the fluidity of the relationship it demands considerable
research and professional skill. It differs from the ordinary conversational
skills used in interpersonal communication in the degree of training that
is needed by the counselor and in the on-the-spot expertise of refining
hypotheses and in constructing multidimensional categories for analysis.

Therapy involves contact between a trained specialist, who
provides the setting and structures the relationship, and a
second person who initiates interaction exclusively to explore
and obtain relief from his emotional problems. Such a relationship is aimed consciously at facilitating change in the
person seeking help (118).

The content of the counseling relationship is the sign-symbol spoken
words which, as a result of actions based on this hypothesis, the counselor is able to make significant for the patron. These "materials"
(words) are composed of gestures, verbal and behavioral, to which the
counselor and the patron respond. The content produced by the counselor's hypotheses is immediately adjusted to the patron's interpretations.
Feedback is almost simultaneous and foreshortens the usual process in
audience-format communications situations where the communicator and
his audience are separated spatially and/or temporally. Consequently,
content analysis of the sign-symbol materials in counseling is an on-
going analysis of what the patron says in order to test hypotheses of the
counselor as to the development of understanding and meaning within
the patron.

Listening is at the heart of context and content analysis in the counseling process. It is upon the basis of his listening analysis that the
counselor forms and focuses his response, the ambiguity or specificity
of his hypotheses, the leading or following of his questions and the depth
of his interpretation. "To be able to listen and to gather information
from another person in this other person's own right, without reacting
along the lines of one's own problems or experiences, of which one may
be reminded perhaps in a disturbing way, is an act of interpersonal exchange which few people are able to practice without special training"
(38).

People who hear do not necessarily listen. The skill of listening
deeply does not develop naturally. Listening to someone talking cannot be redone simply because a speaker cannot be asked to repeat everything he says. Listeners must adjust to the speaker's rate of presentation
and oral communication is frequently not as well organized as written
communication. The speaker's vocabulary cannot easily be checked
against a dictionary. Closer attention is demanded of the listening content analyzer as to "communicator" intentions and "audience" affect
than that demanded of a subject analyst and indexer quietly concentrating
on the technical reading of a document.

Listening appears to be a much more difficult communicative act
than speaking, but even so, listening is only a private experience until
a reply is made. And upon this reply, its nature and scope, hinges
the entire counseling experience for the patron. The counselor's reply
simply has to be based upon a sound hypothesis about the intended meaning
of the patron. For only when the patron recognizes his intended meaning
in the counselor's reply is the accuracy of understanding revealed. Then
and only then does the patron's confidence appear to be justified in terms
of the counsel and advice given by the communicator:

> Opportunity and encouragement to speak must be accompanied
> by motivation to attend to what is being said. This means
> listening without anticipating, without interfering, without
> competing, without refuting, and without forcing meanings
> into preconceived channels of interpretation. It involves a
> sensitive, total concentration on what is explicitly stated
> as well as what is implied by nuances of inflection, phrasing,
> and movement . . . It is not enough to listen if one compre-
> hends only in a detached or intellectual way. It appears to
> be more satisfying and helpful when the listener can partici-
> pate fully in the experience of the speaker, sharing his as-
> sumptions, his values, his motivations — seeing events as
> he sees them. Only through this kind of imaginative sharing
> in the phenomenological world of another person can one really
> sense how events appear to him and how he feels about them
> (14).

A few simulations follow which have been designed for training purposes in interpersonal communication. From a reading of these mini-
ature "case studies", it should be obvious that the patron is heavily involved in real life. Each person apparently has had considerable life
experience and is at the point of a "teachable" moment where guidance
by a helping professional "looks pretty good" to him. However, the
counselor dare not overinterpret or overexpand any of the information
presented by the patron unless he can justify his interpretation:

> Is there an agency or several agencies in this area con-
> cerned with the problem at issue? Could you give directions
> for finding them? Could you give the name of an individual
> to see?
>
> You may only be able to find a source, where the client
> may then in turn be able to obtain further information.

If you have gone as far as you can in obtaining specific
information, project what your next step or the client's
next step would be.

Were you able to make any kinds of judgments about the
referral source?

Keep a record of your thought processes, decisions and
subsequent actions. What experiences did you have and
what were your reactions to those experiences?

Can you give reasons for the referral decisions that you
made?

You may interpret and expand information presented to you
as long as you can justify your interpretations.

Minicases for Interpersonal Communication

Patron is a lonely, frightened, recently-divorced woman with two
children. She asks for information about available groups she might
join to find friendship and support. Where do you send her?

You noticed the patron because she is extremely attractive and well
dressed and is reading Morton Hunt's The Affair. She approaches you
to ask directions but you sense her hesitation to leave, and to your
question, "Can I help in some way?" her eyes fill with tears. Finish
the story and decide on a referral.

Patron is browsing in the Boys' and Girls' room and finally asks for
help in finding easy books that would appeal to an older child. When
you suggest that there is some available material for children with
"learning disability" she is startled. She has never heard that phrase
which seems to describe her child's situation. To whom do you refer
her?

Patron is a middle-aged woman who seems out of place as she sits
at a desk in the psychiatric hospital library which is bustling with students and professionals. She has closed her book on the dynamics of
suicide and is staring into space. She responds to your smile and your
expression of concern by telling you that her husband is acting strangely
and she is trying to find a way to help him. To whom do you refer her?

Patron is a foreign student studying international affairs at the University. He and his young wife have been unable to make friends in their neighborhood. In your conversation you find him to be extremely knowledgeable and witty, but it is difficult to understand his heavily accented English. To whom do you refer him?

Patron is an attractive, late adolescent girl. Her approach to you is made timidly, even sheepishly, and her appearance would indicate profound fatigue and sleeplessness. She asks for the medical section with a note of futility, as though the answers to her questions are not to be found in books. Conversation reveals that the girl is unmarried and pregnant. To whom do you refer her? What are the implications in your choice? How do your own values affect this choice?

Patron is a concerned father whose approach is made boldly and directly. He asks for help in finding an agency that will help his teenage son with a drug problem. The son has dismissed the idea of being admitted to a hospital or of consulting the community mental health agency. To whom do you refer him? What factors made you decide on your decision?

Patron wants to know how to get in touch with a free legal service agency. He is being relocated by the university and feels alone and abandoned in his frustration and anger. He suspects that there are others sharing his feelings but doesn't know how to reach them. You, being a university librarian, have a vested interest in the university's position. To whom do you refer him? What extent does your own stance affect your referral choice?

Patron is depressed, barely verbal (perhaps deficient?), black youth. Conversation reveals him to be out of work, and when he stands up he drags a leg behind him. To whom do you refer him? Why? How far will you go in getting him there?

Patron is an old man whom you have noticed frequently in the reading room pouring over newspapers and news magazines. Today he stares into space and you sit down beside him and start a conversation. He begins to talk about how alone he is, how bored and depressed. What do you do for him?

It is a never ending source of surprise to the independent observer to find that resource specialists in media, library, and information centers are frequently at a loss to know where to turn for community resources and information. Where these simulations are used in in-service training programs, supervisors responsible for staff development may find useful for their purposes the "action bibliography," Where It's At (53). The index to the publication is rather a good place to start with its subject lookup file for community sources and referral. In addition, the following questions may serve for considerations in evaluative sessions:

> Have you listened to the client and allowed the real problem to be revealed? Do you have any feeling that you may not be responding to the real issue?

> Do you feel any responsibility for checking out referral sources? If you do, how do you go about making some evaluation?

> To what extent do your own vested interests, hang-ups, values influence your referral decisions?

> How far will you go in giving support and direction? How much convincing and/or follow through do you feel is appropriate?

What does it feel like to be "disadvantaged" by:

> Unfamiliarity with available community resources.

> Timidity in approaching an unknown voice in an unknown agency (This may be an uncomfortable experience for you — it will be uncomfortable for the client).

> Inability to evaluate the appropriateness or effectiveness of the resource chosen.

COUNSELING INTERFACE

Developmental counseling is aimed at maximizing human freedom. While it may be true that human beings have limited freedom, it is also true that few of them are prepared to exercise what freedom they have. Effective behavior constitutes those human patterns of activity which give man the greatest possible longterm control over his environment as well as the affective responses which are evoked within him by that environment.

The approach known as developmental counseling constitutes an interpersonal relationship in which the communicator serves as a sounding
board in order to assist the patron to help himself. A basic assumption
is that human personality unfolds in terms of an interaction between a
healthy human organism and a professional communicator. Such a
development is seen as a semi-ordered and patterned process of change,
moving in directions that are desirable to the patron. A number of assumptions underlie this approach:

> Patrons are not considered to be "mentally ill" when the
> process is focused upon changing behavior. Patrons are
> considered to be capable of choosing goals, making decisions,
> and generally assuming responsibility for their own behavior
> and future development.

> Developmental counseling is focused on the present and future,
> not the past. Counseling professionals are primarily con-
> cerned over where the patron is going, not where he has been.

> The patron is a person, not a patient. The counselor is not
> an authority figure who follows through with a transference
> relationship that creates the illusion of omnipotence. He
> may be a tutor but is more often a partner as he helps the
> patron move toward his own defined goals.

> The communicator is not morally neutral or amoral. He
> has values, feelings and standards of his own. Although
> he does not impose them on the patron, he nevertheless does
> not attempt to hide them.

> The communicator helps the patron focus upon changing his
> behavior, not just upon intuition and insight. He uses a wide
> variety of techniques within and outside the interview. He
> demonstrates retrieval tasks, arranges tryout experiences,
> and serves as a consultant to the patron based upon a con-
> tinuing relationship.

Counseling is intended to be liberating in nature and aimed at developing responsible independence. Counseling is a planned, systematic
intervention in the life of another human being who is capable of choosing
the desired directions of his own development. The communicator, if
he accomplishes anything, inevitably influences the nature, degree and
direction of behavioral changes that can profit from information surprise

and retrieval. Counseling is much more than advice-giving, although advice may be crucial to the counseling process. It involves more than the answering of a specific question or the solution of an immediate inquiry.

The communicator develops a helping relationship with another person, to contribute in a facilitating, positive way to his improvement. The helping professions engage in activities designed to assist others to understand, to modify, or to enrich their behavior so that growth takes place. Communicators are interested in the information seeking behavior of living, feeling, knowing people as well as in their attitudes, motives, ideas, responses and needs. The helping profession thinks not of individuals as "behavior problems" but as people seeking to articulate and solve the immediate problems of daily life, as well as to feel comfortable about themselves and other people and to meet life's demands productively. The following may serve as characteristics of the helping relationship:

The helping relationship is meaningful because it is personal and intimate, relevant, anxiety-evoking and anxiety-reducing.

Those involved are self-revealing and sensitive to each other. Disclosure of unique and private perceptions and attitudes produces tension and ambiguity. Both cognitive and affective factors are operate; while the emphasis tends to be upon the affective.

Integrity of person is present. Participants intend to be intellectually and emotionally honest with each other.

The helping relationship takes place by mutual consent of the individuals involved. One cannot be compelled to be helpful because duress tears at the fabric of understanding and creates mistrust.

The individual to be helped needs information, instruction, advice, assistance, understanding. The helper exhibits personal charm, skill and energy, or perceptiveness in order to sustain trust. The individual to be helped believes that he will sometime be left in a better position than he was before.

The helping relationship is conducted through communication
and interaction and structure is evident. Both search for
contributions and resources useful in attaining the goal. The
helper puts his skills and information at the disposal of the
other while simultaneously working toward freeing and supporting
the individual's selective powers of initiative. This makes for
collaborative effort, and the one helped feels free to reject
skills, suggestions or contributions which seem inappropriate.

The helping person is approachable and secure. Others feel
free to draw close to him. He is accepting of others, their
ideas, actions, suggestions. He exhibits steadiness and stab-
ility in the relationship.

Change is the object of the helping relationship. The participants
learn from each other, and the experience results in change.
Internal and external change occurs in attitudes, actions, and
perceptions of self, others and world.

In order to give purposeful guidance to patrons, the communicator
will need to understand the psychology of individuals and have a basic
theory of counseling. Some useful assumptions can be borrowed from
the existentialists (8):

The individual is responsible for his own actions. He has
a measure of choice and must make choices for himself.
Since the patron has begun a program of self-improvement
or self-study, he already has indicated that he is willing to
make choices.

Man must regard his fellow man as objects of value, as
part of his own concern. Since his fellow men are part
of him, he must apply his concern to all of society.

Man exists in a world of reality. Much of what he encounters cannot be changed.

He has his own heredity and experiences and will behave
as an individual.

He reacts as a total organism to any situation and will not
react intellectually or emotionally to the exclusion of the
other.

The communicator will take many variant factors into consideration while working with a patron.   This then, presupposes that the professional person will have had training in counseling as part of his educational background or experiences.   He will need to have an opportunity to develop, test and modify his own personal theory and those applications with which he feels comfortable.   Simulation sessions in which he can participate as patron and as counselor will help him become sensitive to others and develop a thorough understanding of himself.   Rogers has developed a client centered approach to counseling that is amenable to media, library, and information science (118):

> The client-centered approach is based upon a psychology of
> learning called "perceptual field theory."   Very briefly,
> the approach holds that all behavior is the function of an in-
> dividual's perceptions at the moment of behaving.   In other
> words, people behave according to how things seem to them.
> Those aspects of the environment to which an individual is
> reacting are called his perceptual field.   This perceptual
> field has the quality of reality to the individual and is always
> organized with respect to the concepts he holds of himself.
> As perceptions change, so too, does behavior.   When people
> perceive differently, they behave differently.   Where per-
> ceptions are vague, behavior is vague.   Where perceptions
> are clear and accurate, behaviors are precise and effective.

The goals of counseling, then, are to assist the client in changing his perceptions and thus activate the behavioral cycle.   There are many different approaches to counseling but there are certain common elements in all models:

> Involves a human relationship.   The counselor must focus
> most of his attention on the quality of that relationship.
>
> Involves some formulation of goals and outcomes.   The
> counselor cannot be a valueless do-gooder who simply wants
> to help people in some abstract sense.
>
> Methods include some process for conceptualizing human
> behavior such as the behaviorizing of message space.
>
> All approaches require some set of skills, competencies,
> sensitivities, and attitudes on the part of the counselor.

Obviously, the value of a theory lies in its usefulness not only for research purposes but especially in guiding the actual counselor-patron interface. In order to do so, the techniques employed should be designed to activate the behavioral cycle in the patron. Rogers has indicated some questions which may be asked in order to facilitate the theory-application transformation (118):

How does the theory deal with the process of human development?

How does the theory explain the nature of human learning?

Does the theory deal with individual differences?

Does the theory offer some central set of constructs or principles for organizing and explaining behavior?

The counselor should evaluate his performance in simulated situations before he approaches the counseling relationship. He must be secure within himself, dependable, consistent, and able to express himself unambiguously. He must be able to accept people and understand why any person has the feelings which he has.

Is the counseling role implied by this theory one that I can assume?

Are the techniques and understandings required by this approach ones that I can master?

Are the goals recommended by this theory ones with which I can comfortably identify?

One of the most basic skills involved in the counseling interview is the task of listening. Most people have learned to become selective listeners. People tune out things they do not want to hear, or automatically reject certain things they have heard. The counselor will react to an expression of feeling rather than ignore it. He will respond to negative feelings in order to change them to positive feelings. Even breathing heavily, blushing, postural changes, and facial expression may change the line of questioning.

Interpersonal communication as a professional method has been developed for, and related to the social objectives of media, library, and information science (104). The publication, Advisory Counseling (103), has further explicated this professional method and placed the counseling interview within reach of professional staff by exploring the skills and techniques which can be acquired by inservice training. Jennerich (66) has researched the preservice training needs of graduate library school students.

COUNSELING INTERVIEW

The interview should be so conducted as to be a helping experience for the patron. The communicator, as a facilitator, promotes patron self-development by bringing congruence between the affective and cognitive domains. Acceptance of all human beings regardless of their behavior means interest in and concern for the client. It does not mean that the communicator has to approve of any particular moral judgement. Empathy involves psychological understanding (cognition) as well as an effective component of feeling. Buckheimer (20) considers the following components as the dimensions of empathy:

Tone: An expressive and often nonverbal dimension based upon nuances of warmth and spontaneity.

Pace: Appropriateness and togetherness of timing in the interview.

Perception: Ability of the counselor to abstract the core of the client's concerns and to formulate them in acceptable terms to him.

Strategy: Predictive or role-playing aspect of the interview.

Leading: Relates to the resourcefulness of the counselor in formulating a set of leads that will move the interview in the direction of the client's concern.

A successful interview requires a manner that is approachable and unhurried, ability to question without seeming to pry or prod, judgement in assessing the patron's level and interest, adaptability in approaching patrons with different backgrounds, and familiarity with the resources (56). It is also necessary to understand the psychological make-up of the patron and how he reacts to his environment. This knowledge can only come by individual contact with the patron. The counselor therefore must be willing to become involved with the patron, and take the

time to ground himself in the behavioral cycle of the specific patron with
whom he is actually in interface.

Since patrons seldom reveal what they are after with their first
questions, the communicator must have sensitivity to unspoken needs.
Close observation of the patron's reactions and gestures may reveal
more to the professional than the spoken word. The counselor needs
skill in helping the patron identify descriptive and factual information
without too much emphasis on self-analysis. The objective is to provide
professional support to the patron while trying to realize the following
characteristics (119):

> Open to his experiences; not defensive or resistant to those
> aspects of his environment that might produce change. All
> aspects of his environment are available to him in the form
> of accurate, realistic perceptions with no built-in barriers.

> Lives in an existential way; he experiences life in terms of
> an ongoing, becoming process. He lives in a fluid stream of
> experience rather than in a rigid or stereotyped way, with an
> absence of tight organization or imposed structure.

> Trusts himself; willing to do that which "feels right," and
> finds his feelings a trustworthy guide to behavior. He has
> the feeling of direction and consistency that flows out of him
> rather than waiting for it to feed in from his environment.

The goal of the interview is not to change the patron's taste and interest, but rather to create a climate in which a change can occur.
Throughout this entire process of interviewing the professional must
preserve an open-mindedness and have the ability to think and act simultaneously and appropriately in any given situation. Professional behavior will vary according to the patron's actual needs and not any pre-
conceived ideas about the needs of the patron.

Since talk is the very basis of the interview, the counselor should
deliberately see to it that the patron does most of the talking and most
of the deciding of what will be talked about. Genuine listening is hard
work. It requires that the counselor not be preoccupied, and also involves hearing the way things are being said, the tones used, the expressions and gestures employed (11). In any event, the following tracking
behaviors (103) will help the counselor think about the components in the
behavioral cycle as he responds to the patron in a professional manner:

Encourage the patron to select the topic for the interview.

Listen for a considerable period of time without commenting.

Seem alert to problems or difficulties other than the first
one mentioned by the patron.

Respond with an economy of words; do not ramble or repeat unnecessarily.

Ask clear and relevant questions, but do not use a standard
catalog of questions.

Use a wide variety of leads to help the patron talk about
his situation.

Phrase questions in an open-ended manner which cannot be
answered yes or no. Why and how rather than what and when.

Follow abrupt shifts in topic by the patron and seem able
to tie these into a common theme.

Where pertinent, restate content of patron's statements,
and endeavor to reflect feelings of the patron.

Usually wait during silences for the patron to respond; do
not interrupt or overtalk the patron or rush the pace of the
interview.

Phrase summaries or interpretations of patron statements in
tentative ways inviting patron feedback. What do you mean;
why does patron hear it this way?

Through control of the resource of his own behavior, the professional provides an existential answer to the following question: "How
can I provide a relationship which this person may use for his own personal growth?" If the professional can provide this relationship, the
other person (patron) will discover within himself the capacity to use
that relationship for growth, change and personal development. This
general hypothesis offers exciting possibilities for the development of
the creative, adaptive and autonomous individual citizen.

This type of relationship is a "helping relationship" (11), and may be defined as a relationship in which at least one of the parties has the intent of promoting in the other growth, development, maturity, improved functioning and coping with life. The other, in this sense, may be an individual or a group. To put it another way, a helping relationship might be defined as one in which one of the participants intends that there should come about, in one or both parties more appreciation of, more expression of, and more functional use of the latent inner resources of the individual. Then the patron in the relationship will:

Experience and understand aspects of himself which previously he has repressed

Find himself becoming better integrated, more able to function effectively

Become more similar to the person he would like to be

Be more self-directing and self-confident

Become more of a person, more unique and more self-expressive

Be more understanding, more accepting of others

Be able to cope with the problems of life more adequately and more comfortably.

The communicator's goal is to provide the atmosphere that will prove most conducive to communication. As interviewer, the professional must be able to accept and understand the patron on his own terms. This acceptance means treating the patron as an equal and regarding his thoughts and feelings with sincere respect. The counselor does not have to agree with the patron's feelings or thinking, but he must be able to understand the patron's life in terms of his ideas, feelings and values. Communicating this to the patron in a sincere manner requires an understanding of the behavioral cycle.

Interpersonal involvement between the counselor and the patron does not mean using the interview to force him into using material in which he has absolutely no interest. The purpose is only to try and create conditions where human change might take place.

If resource specialists possess these qualities plus an open personality, they can confidently attempt to bring better understanding of change in the patron. It is up to each individual professional to take the time to become involved. Skill in various interpersonal techniques is not a substitute for a proper attitude toward the interview, and especially the patron being interviewed. Hence, Johnson's statement (67) many years ago is still worth observing today:

> No readers advisor will ever be good for more than half a
> dozen serious interviews a day. Even this would be too much
> if it were a daily affair, because the readers advisor needs
> time for making at least sketchy records, for preparing lists,
> and above all for keeping up with the literature.

INTERVIEWING TECHNIQUES

There are a variety of utterances (questions, statements, nonverbals) which have in common the quality of conveying the interviewer's own perceptions or dispositions relatively directly: reassurance, surprise, expressions of interest. The following categories can be employed for the purposes of analysis, measurement and evaluation:

Truth-Value: Utterances which both propose the existence
of certain facts and signal the patron to confirm or deny the
truth of the proposition.

Restatement: Utterances which repeat the content of previous counselor messages. Restatements signal that the message has been received and that the interviewer is attempting
to clarify it. It also implies that his information on the topic
is uncertain or incomplete.

Datum: Utterances which signal incompleteness of information on relatively concrete topics as supplied by the patron.
No proposition is asserted.

Open End: Utterances which signal incompleteness of information on abstract topics or which leave the topics relatively
unspecified. As with the datum, no proposition is asserted.

Content: Utterances which are directed at the patron's knowledge of "objective fact."

Feeling: Utterances which are directed at the patron's personal perceptions, attitudes and values.

An important aspect of counseling is the technique of question-asking.
In preparing questionnaires, surveys and other fact gathering devices
the goal is usually to obtain the desired facts in the least ambigious form.
But in resource counseling, data gathering is not the goal but only a means
to an end. However, many of the basic considerations of the survey interview are applicable to the question asking process in the counseling
interview.

Open questions are more likely to be used in the beginning
of an inquiry-negotiation, that is until the librarian and
patron together understand enough about the subject of concern. Responses to open questions help to lay out a general
map of the patron's inquiry and thus reveal relevant avenues
for search strategy. As the inquiry negotiation progresses,
closed questions produce more relevant and specific responses,
i.e., establish a greater degree of congruity between the
patron's felt need and his overt request (110).

After rapport has been established, the interview should begin with
easy questions that do not pry, embarrass, invoke negative attitudes
or confuse the patron. Only one question should be asked at a time.
If there is no response, or if the response has no relevancy to the question being discussed, the question can be rephrased. Questions should
be so constructed that they are easily understood. It goes without saying
that one does not phrase questions in professional jargon. To say to a
patron, "Which bibiliographical tools have you tried?" can cause a negative reaction. The person may be too embarrassed or too confused
to say, "What do you mean by a bibliographical tool?"

No question should imply its own answer. Questions which require
only a "yes" or "no" answer may result in a situation where the interviewer does most of the talking. As a result, the patron will feel he is
being interrogated. The patron should be able to qualify his answers
and easily advance into the next point of discussion. The interviewer
may have to repeat the patron's answer to be sure that he understands
what the patron really meant to say. How the patron interprets the
question is the significant determinant. It is the patron's viewpoint that
is important.

There is a place in the interview for the closed question. Closed questions can lead to specificity as well as congruity between the felt need that drove the person into the resource center and the overt expression which provides a basis for negotiation. There should be some balance between the open and closed questions. Open questions help the patron to express his need and do not impose on him a feeling of rigidity. Closed questions indicate to the patron that the communicator has been listening to previous statements. The well-informed patron is usually willing to answer the open-end question in order to reveal his knowledge and thus impress the librarian.

On the other hand, the patron who has little knowledge about the subject being discussed does not want to reveal any inadequacy. He would prefer to make short, noncommital answers. The experienced interviewer should be able to detect the effects of open and closed questions. From feedback, whether verbal or physical, he can decide whether the patron is irritated by closed questions or more comfortable with open questions.

As the interview progresses antecedent questions can be employed. These questions enable the interviewer to use an earlier response as a starting-point for a new approach and thus increase respondent participation. Antecedents are particularly valuable in clarifying an earlier statement. If the immediate prior response has been relevant the interviewer can use the echo. This is a mere repetition of the patron's last remark and has the affect of keeping him talking on the same subject.

If the patron seems to be losing his trend of thought, a summary may be useful. The summary must be carefully handled. It may be an actual summary of what the patron really said. It should not include any interviewer interpretation. Otherwise, the patron may agree to a summary which would otherwise be a distortion.

Leading questions may be necessary in some interviews. The two components of leading questions are expectation and premise. The librarian may use expectations where he is certain that a valid answer will more firmly motivate the patron toward continued self-improvement. In the expectation, the expected answer is evident:

If the interviewer asks, "Are you a library borrower?" he does not indicate the answer he expects. The question can be answered by "yes" or "no". It is not an expectation. If, however, he asks, "You are a library borrower, aren't you?" he clearly indicates that he expects a "yes" answer.

Many nonverbal encouragements may be used in interviewing which
help to break up and space an otherwise continuous flow of verbal exchange. Silences of reasonable length usually produce further responses.
A brief pause to think through his answers may help the patron become
more willing to talk or to rephrase what he has said in more valid statements. A smile, a nod or just the fact of sitting up in attention may cause
the patron to continue talking.

The "guggle" on the other hand sometimes has the opposite effect.
The guggle usually as a nonverbal sound has the effect of changing the
pattern of thought, or of keeping a too loquacious person from running
on forever. The "guggle" may be just "Ah", indicating that the interviewer would like to interrupt. If this does not work, a beginning word
may be necessary.

DISCOURSE ANALYSIS

An extension refers to a response made earlier in the interview.
It can be used to get the patron to talk more freely and thus increase
the scope of response upon which eventually the search strategy can be
built. However, if a patron shows resistance, the communicator not
knowing whether the resistance is due to the patron's lack of information
(or interest) or to feelings of anxiety (insecurity or threat), may move
on to another question. Later, when the patron appears more confident
and at ease, the interviewer can return to the earlier topic and, through
an extension, attempt to obtain the coverage that was not obtained earlier.

The echo is an exact (or nearly exact) repetition of the patron's
words by the communicator generally with a rising inflection at the end
of his question. If used effectively, the echo makes the patron feel that
the counselor is following him closely and sympathetically and is encouraged to continue to express himself freely. The silence also can be
used to uncover new information, because the patron after a silence may
continue talking. Like the echo, the silence may have little or no effect
on the patron's line of thought.

Unlike the extension, the echo is employed only when the prior response is relevant. It encourages the patron to continue with little or
no change in his subject. It is useful only when the counselor feels that
the patron has more to say on the same subject. The use of encouragement has a similar effect. But if the echo is used when he has exhausted
the question, it may sound silly or irritating, and hence, may lower the
level of participation.

The clarification is a request for clarification, specification, or elaboration of ambiguous, vague, or implicit statements made in a prior part of the interview. For example, clarification may be open: "What did you mean when you said . . . ?"' or closed: "Did you decide to go or didn't you?" A clarification may also be used to obtain depth: "Why did this upset you?"

There are two kinds of clarification. In direct clarification, the counselor specifically requests information about a general, vague or ambiguous prior response. In inferential clarification, the counselor makes an explicit inquiry about information, which remains buried in a prior part of the interview. The inferential clarification has been most fully used in nondirective counseling. There, the interviewer pays close attention to the feelings implicit in the respondent's statements and then asks a question designed to clarify and make explicit the implicit content.

A summary is a question which summarizes information previously given by the patron and (explicitly or implicitly) requests confirmation or correction. The summary assembles, consolidates, and synthesizes pieces of information which the patron has provided in discrete responses. It gives significance and relevance to the response material. It can clarify ambiguities. Also, without hurting feelings, it can cut short a patron who tends to be garrulous or discursive. Consequently, the counselor has a way of increasing his control over the interview whenever this becomes necessary in order to expedite the attainment of purpose.

The summary gives the interviewer greater control because it is a closed question and requires only brief affirmation as a response. But it shares with the closed question the danger of yea-saying. It is always easier for a patron to agree with a summary than to disagree and specify why he disagrees. The patron may feel shy about disagreeing or feel that his disagreement casts aspersions on the intelligence or ability of the counselor. This danger is serious if the summary is used to clarify ambiguous information. More damaging, however, to potential self-learning by the patron is the practice of some librarians to develop their own summaries (which incorporate distortions) and subsequently attribute such distortion to the respondent.

The confrontation may be used sparingly but only with those patrons who have a measure of self-confidence. The counselor may note inconsistency within a response, between two discrete responses, or between a response and another source of information presumed to be accepted by the patron. At this point he may use a confrontation — that is, a question which presents the patron with the inconsistency and asks for its resolution. The confrontation is used to increase validity, specificity, or clarity and congruity.

Because confrontation is best known in the courtroom as the cross-examination of witnesses, it has connotations of badgering and threatening. However, this need not always be the case, especially when the tone of voice and facial behavior is empathetic and sincere. A confrontation may be regarded as an indicating of the counselor's sincere interest and careful attention. In any event, the interviewer needs to weigh carefully the consequences of a confrontation upon the participation of the respondent.

A repetition is a question which merely repeats a question previously asked. This device should be used sparingly as it may irritate the patron and suggest that the communicator is either inexperienced or inattentive. In general, repetitions are rarely used. Many of the purposes they serve can be served as well, if not better by varying the wording of the questions in order to approach the earlier content of the interview from a slightly different perspective.

In summary, various types of questions as the product of the discourse between patron and reference librarian have been analyzed by Vavrek (146). This approach has long been under consideration by the profession (120) and other analyzes have been made (88, 141). Caruso (25) and Williams (153) have placed the process of content analysis and the resulting interactive protocols within the framework of information science. Other evaluative devices such as interaction analysis and non-verbal critiques are available (103).

Evaluation is based upon the understandings and competencies required by the resource specialist in media, library, and information science in order to engender the surprise value of information within the patron (104). This objective is accomplished by activating the behavioral cycle in the patron and following through with articulation and description as well as problem analysis, solution, prediction and application. Sample interviews have been analyzed (110) and a number of rating scales have been employed to measure professional behavior (103).

THREE

ADVOCACY GUIDANCE

Advisory services constitute a method of guidance which can be employed with patrons who have already articulated their perceptions of some life situation in which they are involved. The urge or feeling of dissatisfaction which motivated the patron to participate in an interpersonal encounter with the communicator has been expressed. But the patron is not entirely at ease either with himself or the dimensions of knowledge which have been opened up by the communicator. He feels the need of a self tutorial program in reading, viewing and listening experiences which can be prescribed by the communicator. This type of service has been traditionally called "readers" advisory or bibliotherapy.

The counselor on the other hand is a person to whom a patron comes to get a fresh and different perspective about himself and his concerns. The major emphasis in counseling is not primarily upon any information that is to be imparted, but upon aiding of the individual toward self-motivation and self-decision. It is developmental in character. The first job of the counselor is to gain the patron's confidence, and to try to understand him as a whole person.

Under ordinary conditions, the counselor may next work toward enabling the patron to understand himself in relation to his environment and toward the setting up of self-reliant, problem solving, heuristic attitudes within him. When the patron is prepared for it, the counselor will undertake to retrieve the necessary information himself; whereas on other occasions he may only suggest where it can be found and how it might be used. On other occasions he will find it necessary to give guidance of one kind or another, perhaps in relation to the means of obtaining specific types of information, or possibly with respect to their application to the patron's particular problems.

HISTORICAL PERSPECTIVE

The professional helping relationship of the resource change agent, at least in its modern phase, was not discussed seriously until the 1876 Report on Libraries of the U. S. Office of Education which included a collection of papers about libraries and library service. Two papers by Perkins and Matthews (111) developed the function of the "professor of books" who was to be an expert in resources and an agent for change in human development. Over the years, this particular aspect of inter-personal communication has received impetus in the individualized and group training programs of the "library college" movement (19, 131).

The influence of the 1876 Report on the professional helping aspects of librarianship was considerable. For example, Maddox (89) in analyzing the first ten years of the proceedings of the American Library Association found that considerable attention was given to the function of the change agent in a resource center. The essential elements were identified and the roles of the resource agent in this helping relationship were developed at least in prototype and remain largely unchallenged today. During the first years of the Library Journal, Green (48) wrote extensively on the subject and has often been called the "father" of professional resource service to the individual. Green laid the basis for this helping relation-ship. The skills of this type of resource agent include not only a listening ear and receptive mind but also a deep and wide knowledge of classification, materials selection and information retrieval, once the patron has been helped to identify his request:

> But having acquired a definite notion of the object concerning
> which information is desired, the habit of mental classification,
> which a librarian acquires so readily, comes to his aid. He
> sees at once in what department of knowledge the description
> sought for may be found, and brings to the inquirer authorit-
> ative treatises in this department.

In Green's mind, the change agent should be placed at the point of first contact with the patron and from this vantage point could listen to the perhaps halting and often inchoate ramblings of individual citizens. Through interviewing, the resource agent could help the patron bring some order out of his confusion before negotiating possible strategies for retrieval, whether outside the agency to appropriate resources in the nonverbal and audiovisual message space of the people, or referral to the subject specialists within the resource center (48):

> In the case of such persons, as well as with scholars, it is
> practicable to refer applicants for information you cannot
> supply to libraries in larger cities in the neighborhood of
> your own library, or to other institutions in your own town.
> Businessmen go to commercial centers so often that they can
> occasionally consult larger libraries than those accessible at
> home.

If the patron needed further assistance he was then provided with the necessary resources; or the resource agent could provide the actual information in whatever form desired by the patron for his particular purposes. The change agent stood ready to access all possible resources to meet the patron's need and even, when necessary, to transfer the reader to subject specialists within the agency, or to professionals in other fields outside the center without undermining the reader's sense of continuity in the helping relationship.

On these foundations, the work of the resource agent was explicated over the years in three areas which were considered to be essential to the functional effectiveness of a resource change agent. These areas were: (1) selection and classification; (2) bibliography and reference; and (3) interpersonal relations. The first two areas were developed more explicitly than the third because of their integral function in the profession of media, library, and information science which had been under development for centuries. These areas are today the basis of work in advisory counseling, media therapy, reference retrieval and training laymen in the use of a wide range of knowledge and other information sources.

In reviewing the services of resource centers in his day, Johnson (67) evaluated the effectiveness of the professional's helping relationship. Consultation was provided and advice given about materials selection and reference strategies, but Johnson made a special plea for a better understanding of, and training of resource agents in interpersonal communication. It was in this area that Johnson felt a professional discipline could be expanded, and be of considerable value to the continuing self-educational development of a large segment of the population in any community. However, since no rational foundation in the philosophy of counseling or education has been developed in the profession, the prescriptions identified by Johnson have rarely gone beyond the platitudes of a social etiquette which are summarized, for example, in the librarian's manual for interpersonal relations known as Patrons are People (147). A more recent statement puts the matter in contemporary perspective: "The librarians themselves have not realized that an essential element in professional behavior is clientele service based on expertise and on the willingness to do all that is involved in order to assume the role of expert (100)."

Resource specialists have always had at least a vocal appreciation of, and some respect for the individual patron and his needs for information and communication. Both their guidance and educational functions

have been based on pragmatic methods of communication which have
been developed over the years into what may now appear to be a vocational
method of communication. Two early statements by leaders in the profession give evidence of some continuing concern for interpersonal communication and educational development:

> We must first interest the reader before we can educate
> him; and to this end, must commence at his own standard
> of intelligence (112).

> Both teachers and librarians have united in careful study of
> the child's natural development, in selecting courses of
> reading for him, in devising methods for encouraging his
> own powers of research (150).

Statements such as these and others over the years with a similar
orientation anticipate the developmental counseling of a Carl Rogers and
the educational psychology of a John Dewey. However, perhaps because
of their humanistic origins and preoccupations, resource specialists
have not developed their insights into a theory of communication and
have not been particularly receptive to theoretical disciplines and social
science methods of inquiry. It is a curious syndrome whereby, as if
by accepting a scientific discipline, the profession would lose its unique
identity as a humanistic endeavor which promotes the reading of books
as the method par excellence for the attainment of the good life.

While the resource profession has not incorporated any formal
theory in its professional deliberations about the helping relationship
between patron and agents, much work has been undertaken in what
Dickoff (30) calls "a reporting of what somebody took to be the salient
features of some situation." Libraries in Adult Education (1) appeared
in 1924 and thoroughly explored the role of the resource agent in adult
education. This survey report examined various aspects of the resource
specialist's role in continuing informal education and reaffirmed the
important role of interpersonal communication in helping patrons prepare
themselves for effective participation in group and community communicative experiences. This participative function was later rationalized
and explicated for educational communications by Gagne (42) as one of
the basic conditions for more effective learning.

In the 1930s and 1940s a serious effort was made to develop the re-
commendations for interpersonal relations of the 1924 Report by such
leaders as John Chancellor, Jennie Flexner and Miriam Thompkins.

Exploiting professional work done in resource selection and classification, as well as bibliographic and reference retrieval for human purposes, these leaders developed a range of interpersonal communication skills. They were supported in the endeavor by the work of Merrill (93) who developed a code based on a problem-solving model which users and classifiers could use to interface productively. Somewhat later, Hutchins (64) worked out the rationale and function of counseling for resource specialists, while Shores (130) developed a method of thinking which users and professional agents could employ for individual and personal cognitive development and cognitive flexibility.

The importance of these models of thinking and their function in educational communication and counseling were later explicated by Belth (10). Dale (29), as the father of educational communications, broadened both the resource base to include all the artifacts of man as well as the professional function of materials creation and production. Haines (51) localized the principles of content analysis of resource materials in the historical accretion of broad subject fields. The work of Haines complemented the results which were already available from the "geography of reading" studies (155) of the Chicago Graduate Library School. The confluence of these two intellectual endeavors helped to make the principles of materials selection and classification not only kinetic in the lives of people but also related to some concept of maturity in self-education through reading, viewing and listening. Later, Asheim (6) was able to summarize and rationalize the role of the librarian in communication under two headings: content analysis and audience research.

In 1954, Maxfield (91) reported on the first serious attempt to integrate and rationalize the function of interpersonal communication based upon research findings in related and other pertinent fields of inquiry. Maxfield maintained that change agent communication differs significantly from data retrieval and advisement, as well as such tutorial and instructional aspects of the resource center included under the generic heading, Training Layman in the Use of the Library (17). Advisement, information transfer and instruction are one-way communication processes where the resource agent tells the patron the most efficient way of reaching his goal.

The resource change agent, on the other hand, encourages the patron to assume initiative and responsibility in evaluating his feelings, the facts of his situation and the cognitive analysis and symbolization of his experience. In addition to the communicative methods appropriate to his role, the resource change agent employs the techniques of the

information specialist and the media adviser. Such creative and critical
problem-solving techniques include resource browsing and audiovisual
composition. The encouragement of materials browsing among patrons
is the major method of the advisory counselor, while the composition
of themes in audiovisual materials is at the core of media therapy and
communication.

It may be contended by some professionals in the media, library,
and information specializations that a behavioral approach has been
taken to their service programs. They are, of course, correct, in
part, in this perception, but they do indeed need to be reminded that
the standards by type of agency (media, library, or information center)
are oriented more to institutional systems (59) than primarily to human
beings. Unfortunately, much of the literature of service to the individual
is preoccupied with the manipulation of things, such as materials, bibliographies, or facilities and equipment rather than the design of situations within which communicative activity can occur (Table 2).

PATRON INTRAPERSONAL CONCERNS

Intrapersonal communication in a resource center presents many
problems. Although one might expect the scope of problems and the
range of abilities to be limited, often the reverse is true. Age has
very little relevance to mental ability. The resource specialist must
be prepared to offer materials covering the entire spectrum of interests and abilities including advanced adult materials as well as very elementary level materials with high interest factors. The range of materials sought are not limited to any subject area.

Often the patron comes to the center seeking "what" he should read,
while in reality he wants to know "how" to read and needs to be instilled
with the desire to read. It is often difficult for some librarians to be
aware of the socioeconomic, educational and cultural differences between
himself and his patrons. The patron who can see absolutely no desir-
ability or advantage in books or reading can hardly be expected to seek
out the librarian to ask for reading guidance. He is unaware that a
problem exists or that the specialist is there for his benefit. He may
believe that her only purpose is to police the area to keep it free of
harmful offenders.

The ability to recognize the structure of a written message appears
to be positively correlated with both listening comprehension and reading
comprehension. In addition to the recognition of standard sentence

Table 2

Behavior-Service Relationship

Cycle of Behavior	Service
Articulate and describe visceral need.	Developmental Counseling
Identify avenues that might be taken (opportunity set).	Articulation
State preferences in opportunity set (goals).	Description
SR to lay out subject imbedded in initial concern and opportunity set.	Advisory Guidance
RR to dig out facts and relationships.	Reference Retrieval
IR for opinions, conclusions relevant to the way others have solved similar problems.	Information Retrieval
Message design a speech or program.	Group Dynamics
Assemble audience (Who and Whats).	Decision Making
Create action, obtain legislation and budget.	Prediction and Action

patterns, the effective listener notes the pattern of presentation which includes the central idea, subordinate and supporting points, the analysis and the generalization. Librarians have probably always recognized the importance of knowing the intrapersonal skills of communication. But they have not always been aware of them and have not deliberately planned to include continuous improvement in reading, viewing and listening as an imperative instructional element in every advisory counseling communication.

The principles of maturity in reading apply as well to listening and viewing. Much more time is spent exercising viewing and listening skills which, however, are not any less difficult to learn if critical and creative thinking are to be pursued. It is not difficult to appreciate and realize the application of these characteristics as sought-for objectives of any media learning experience (47):

A genuine enthusiasm for reading.

Tendency to read: (a) a wide variety of materials that contribute pleasure, widen horizons, and stimulate creative
thinking; (b) serious materials which promote a growing
understanding of one's self, of others, and of problems of
a social, moral, and ethical nature; and (c) intensively in
a particular field relating to a central core.

Ability to translate words into meanings, to secure a clear
grasp and understanding of the ideas presented, and to sense
clearly the mood and feelings intended.

Capacity for and habit of making use of all that one knows
or can find out in interpreting the meaning of the ideas
read.

Ability to perceive strengths and weaknesses in what is
read, to detect bias and propaganda, and to think critically
concerning the validity and values of the ideas presented and
the adequacy and soundness of the author's presentation,
views, and conclusions. This involves an emotional apprehension, either favorable or unfavorable, as well as a
penetrating intellectual grasp of what is read measured on
some scale of comprehension.

Tendency to fuse the new ideas acquired through reading
with previous experience, thus acquiring new or clear
understandings, broadened interests, rational attitudes,
improved patterns of thinking and behaving, and richer
and more stable personalities.

Capacity to adjust one's reading pace to the needs of the
occasion and to the demands of adequate interpretation.

The following sets of criteria have been added for listening and then
for viewing in order to exhibit the ease with which this transformation
can be made. Because a person is hearing something does not mean
that he is listening — just as seeing is not reading. It is difficult to
think independently while listening to a speaker. While going off on your
own thoughts you may miss several of the next points made. A person
may hear what the communicator says and yet not listen in any of these
four ways:

Purposefully; to gain information, to make life more
enjoyable.

Accurately; speakers to not need to scream nor to repeat
themselves constantly if participants are to listen intently.

Critically; think of what Hitler did to his listeners.

Responsively; those numbers in football call for a certain
action; so does an explanation of behavior.

Motivation is important in all types of learning. Learning to listen
is no exception. Just as a real interest in and desire for reading is the
most important factor in teaching reading so must we develop a need for
listening. A patron develops little need for critical listening when the
advisor continually talks:

Listening for enjoyment and appreciation (to oral reading
and speaking):

Enjoy the development of a story or the surprise of
a joke.

Listen for tuneful words and pleasing rhythm.

Visualize descriptive and dramatic passages.

React to the mood set by an author.

Appreciate a speaker's or writer's (oral reading)
style.

Be aware of the favorable or unfavorable effects of
voice, posture, or gestures.

Note how character is revealed through dialog.

Listening for information and for specific purposes:

For the answer to a specific question.

Follow directions, step by step.

Reproduce what is said, as in a message.

Follow sequence in a story, play or demonstration

Listen for main ideas, for detail — descriptive, supplementary.

Relate details to respective main points.

Take running notes which reflect the speaker's outline.

Interpret new words through context.

Listening to criticize and evaluate:

Distinguish between the truth and rationalization.

Discriminate between fact and opinion.

Listen for evidence which supports a speaker's statement.

Detect prejudice and bias.

Evaluate propaganda by a check against observable facts.

Recognize sales-pressure techniques.

Sense a speaker's purpose.

Viewing which has not been integrated into intrapersonal communication more often lulls one's mind than arouses the anxiety so necessary to the processes of critical thinking. Unless carefully organized in an educative sequence, visuals will confuse rather than lead the mind to abstract and to generalize. Viewing experiences are largely programmed sequences which come to the individual through mass media and other projection equipment. Occasions seldom if ever arise to stop the sequence and pause for reflection and comparison. Questions such as the following may prove helpful in reflecting on the viewing experience:

For whom and for what purpose was the visual sequence
produced?

Are the sponsor and producer recognized as responsible
persons in this area of programming; or, are sensational
scenes and sounds sought for their own sake?

Does the presentation have a theme; or, is it lost in
visual detail and obscured by the sound track?

Have scenes been selected from irrelevant visualization
for sequential effect?

What is the relation of verbal to nonverbal content? For
what purpose and function are the captions employed?

Considerable emphasis has traditionally been placed on the verbal
retrieval skills in the cognitive domain. Obviously this imbalance is a
result of the place which knowledge production, storage and retrieval
has in western civilization. It is also evident from the fact that while
the library was early established as a publicly supported social agency
for the distribution of one medium of communication, nothing comparable
exists for the other media. For example, the products of radio and
television are not preserved let alone distributed after their initial appearance. Part of the reason may be attributed to misplaced values,
but of more significance is the fact that audiovisual and nonverbal composition is a major and dynamic component of a happening. It is the
function of a "happening" in part to teach the skills of listening and
viewing in order to effectively probe for hidden intentions in the affective domain.

Such an objective has only recently become a responsibility of
specialists in information, library, and media science and use of the
center for this purpose must also be taught to patrons. The imperative
is all the more pressing since audiovisual composition is not taught in
schools and colleges. The emphasis is almost exclusively on verbal
composition which is largely logical in design. Audiovisual composition
on the other hand is involved with the juxtaposition of images, sounds
and movements based on nonverbal and largely intuitive meaning within
the affective domain. Audiovisual communication is to some extent
verbally inchoate and is closely related to an informal level of communication.

The professional recognizes that his objective in all community planning is to increase the participation of the community in the benefits of knowledge.

Frequently advisory personnel suffer from the confusion which exists
between the sense that their responsibility is to provide only the information asked for and their assumption that their purpose is to educate
the user in how to find the information for himself. Actually guidance
is the primary focus of the service; materials and the media center are
but the channels of communication. The functions of advisory personnel
are to serve the patron by (95):

Providing authentic, pertinent and adequate information
about vocations, educational opportunities, social relationships, and personal development.

Assisting the individual in locating and interpreting information pertinent to problem solving.

Aiding the individual in orienting and adjusting to educational
opportunities, especially those available through the library.

Assisting in obtaining information which will lead to a
better understanding of the individual, and utilizing available
information about the individual in working more effectively
with him.

Providing opportunities through social contacts, assigned
responsibilities, exploring activities, and constructive environment which will lead to greater insights and satisfactory
development of the individual.

Providing such counseling services to the individual as are
in keeping with the operation of the counseling program and
the competency of the librarian.

Patrons do not always ask the question they want to know. In some
instances they cannot define what they want in the terms of a subject,
but they can tell why they want it. This leads them frequently to ask
very specific questions, as if they were afraid to hold up their ignorance
for everyone to see. The hardest part of negotiating a question is frequently not so much finding the answer as finding the question. The
following may serve as possible reasons why patrons do not ask really
pertinent questions from the start of their inquiry (100):

The patron lacks knowledge of the depth and quality of the collection.

The patron lacks knowledge of the reference tools available.

The patron lacks knowledge of the vocabulary used by a particular set of tools.

The patron does not willingly reveal his reason for needing the information.

The patron has not decided what he really wants.

The patron is not at ease in asking his questions.

The patron feels that he cannot reveal the true question because it is of a sensitive nature.

The patron dislikes reference staff members (or vice versa) and consequently avoids giving a true picture of his needs.

The patron lacks confidence in the ability of the reference staff.

CONSTRAINTS AND OPPORTUNITIES

In essence, advisory service is largely the selection of materials for the particular concerns and interests of individual patrons. The communicator through guidance and interpretation assists the patron to select those reading, viewing and listening experiences which are most appropriate to the concerns and interests articulated in the counseling interface. The broad objectives have become prevalent in the profession (133):

Provide opportunities for individuals of any age to select and negotiate reading, viewing and listening experiences relevant to needs and purposes.

Help individuals and groups interpret and apply experiences with reading, viewing and listening to continuing self-control and self-design.

Motivate the unfocused information users to participate in
planned and developmental intrapersonal communication
experiences.

Motivate the random user to pursue the ideas and concepts
which grow out of his life experience through continuing self-
educational programs.

Guide the individual towards maturity in the intrapersonal
communication skills of reading, viewing, listening, resource
and index center use.

Once the librarian has established empathy with his patron, he
must begin to identify the problem. No search of materials can be
begun unless the object of the search can be recognized. If one cannot
recognize what he seeks, how will he know when he has found it? For
this reason, the librarian must be willing and able to communicate effectively. Each person, throughout his entire lifetime, has been gathering
experiences, perceiving stimuli, and forming meanings for words based
upon what his experiences have meant to him. No two lives are identical.
No two people experience exactly the same events or stimuli in exactly
the same order under identical sets of conditions or circumstances.

Consequently, no two people can have identical meanings for the
words they use to express ideas. The librarian is wise who realizes
this fact and tries to establish a rapport with his patron that will enable
him to bring out the values and the basic ideas behind the words he uses.
Only when the librarian is relatively sure that his meanings and those
of his patron are congruent should he proceed with the retrieval stragegy
(Figure 1). If a request is accepted at face value without a discussion
of purposes or needs, much time can be wasted. A quick search may
reveal nothing. A long search may still reveal nothing but the point-
lessness of the search. After it has been completed, the "drops" retrieved may be something entirely foreign to what the patron had in
mind.

In verbal message space, the patron has been able traditionally to
receive two basic services from the agency supported by information,
library, and media science: advisory guidance and reference retrieval.
The difference is one of emphasis rather than kind, and depends upon
the patron's concern or interest. The patron may interface with the
professional catalyst from either of two orientations or with a combination of the two:

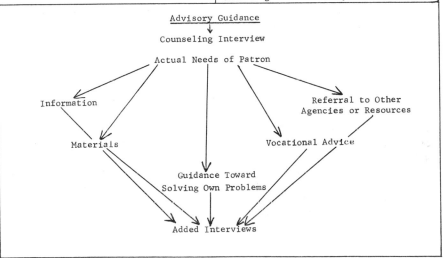

Figure 1. Advisory Guidance

Probably one of the reasons that there is so much confusion
in some librarians' minds as to the proper distinction between
these two kinds of library service, both of which require interest in people combined with bibliographical knowledge, is
that the difference lies less in the librarian and the question

than in the motives of the inquirer which are not always obvious
to the librarian or even to the reader himself. If the inquirer's
prime interest is in producing a change in himself, or, for
cases presented at secondhand, in some person in whom he is
interested, through self-education by means of books, he
should be introduced to the readers adviser. If, on the other
hand, his main interest is in the subject, whether from mental
curiosity or from an intention to make some direct, practical
use of the information he hopes to gain, he should be referred
to the reference department or a subject specialist (64).

Advisory guidance work is directly connected with the concept of
continuing education. From its beginnings, the service was seen as
a center for answering questions related to continuing education and resource centers. Through the years, since its beginnings, in the 1920s,
there have been varying interpretations of just what the service actually
entails. After World War II, however, many people began to realize
the importance of the library in the adult education process. They discovered that in spite of costs and opposition from some people, the library in its very makeup is one of the few public informational services
which is geared to meeting the needs of the individual.

ASSESSMENT AND EVALUATION

Assessment implies the measurement of the extent to which patron
behavior subsequent to guidance is a function of what occurs during the
advisory contact. But with the central problem such as time dynamic
service is hard to evaluate. The patron may have changed merely because he had grown older or had received help from some outside source.
The important factor is the change which can be attributed to the helping
relationship. Much remains to be done on the effectiveness of advisory
guidance with what kind of patron and for what goals. To some degree,
guidance can be evaluated by goal-relevant behavior.

If a person has come to the library for help in planning a
self-study program and he does carry through, finds a
better job, goes on to college, or in some way makes use
of what he has learned, we can say that he did fulfill a commitment to a specified goal.

If he gets good grades, acquires better study habits, or learns
a job skill, he has shown competence. If he has shown consistency in taking the right courses or establishing social affil-
iations he has shown measurable progress.

It is one thing to provide advisory guidance service but it is quite another to determine the effectiveness of such service. Some evaluative processes will be needed to establish whether the patron got what he wanted and whether his awareness has increased of what the resource communicator can do for him should other needs develop. Possibly, the only effective method is the continuous monitoring of his own performance via an unobstrusive videocamera. In any event, the traditional profession has identified a number of evaluative questions (101) without any suggestions for measurement:

Articulation and Description

Does the advisor's conversation with the patron bring out informally his background and interests?

Do you encourage the patron to help evaluate the advice given?

Are your booklists fresh, attractive and distributed outside the agency?

Do exhibits relate material ordinarily separated under regular classification schemes?

Have present groupings of books such as "western", "mysteries", "new books," successfully stimulated use?

Are there other broad areas of interest in the community about which groups of books might be organized?

Retrieval and Referral

Does your talk with the patron acquaint him with message space and the indexes of importance to his particular needs and interests?

What functions do booklists serve in advisory services?

Do you record any facts brought out in the conversation so as to give further help to the patron?

How do you find out if the patron got what he needed?

Do you keep a file of readers' continuing interests?

Do you have a regular system of notifying readers of books which might be of interest to them?

How do you make sure that the patron knows what the library can do for him as other needs develop?

Evaluation and Followup

Do patrons regularly return for more "conversations"?

Do satisfied patrons give you word of mouth publicity?

Has advisory service helped to make the general public think of the agency as more than a mere lending service?

Do you give your board of trustees facts and figures about advisory service so that they can help increase its effectiveness with funds and personnel?

How do you measure the effectiveness of your reader's advisory service?

In summary, with the integration of media, library, and information science, the power of the reference-form model has been strengthened to include audiovisual and nonverbal forms within the totality of message space, that is, the organized collection of materials accessed by the resource agency. From a behavioral and developmental viewpoint, objects, movement, and sound have been added to the traditional reference-form categories and are employed for articulation purposes and audiovisual therapy. Nonverbal objects, movement, and sound when combined into audiovisual compositions and captioned by verbal cues constitute a powerful method by means of which patrons can be intrapersonally supported in the endeavor of problem description, analysis, and specification of a concern or interest.

Content labels or descriptors, and abstracts which are products of professional content analysis, are employed by the inquiry negotiator in an attempt to locate through the reductive transformations of indexing those portions of several communications messages relevant to the patron-initiated inquiry. Counseling content analysis is used by the resource

communicator in a transactional manner to help the patron develop
some cognitive direction in his unorganized everyday experiences. On
the other hand, question negotiation for information retrieval, although
it may utilize the transactional interview, shifts the function of the interaction from cognitive development to cognitive flexibility. This difference occurs as a response to the individual user's entry mode
(Figure 2).

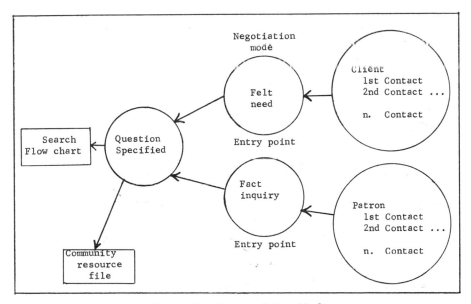

Figure 2 . System Entry Mode

Counseling content analysis listens to meaning as it unfolds in the
interview. It hypothesizes about client intention and direction, and the
applicability of particular communication resources. This type of
content analysis, if it can be called such, investigates the patron's
real life experiences (which are usually unorganized) in an attempt to
dotormino what symbols, if any, may emerge. Once symbolization
occurs, meaningful contact or interface can eventually be established

with some part of the corpus of knowledge. Presumably, this initial
interface with knowledge is investigated further and leads into the information retrieval type of inquiry investigated in the work of the information scientist.

Perceptual input detected as a result of a stimulus from the real
world of sense experience leads to value-selected concepts symbolized
internally within the individual and results externally in the development
of judgements within the context of language. Questions or uncertainties
that may develop at any point in the basic cybernetic behavioral cycle,
have implications for human intercourse and may be investigated in the
negotiation cycle of reliable observation, valid inference and logical
discourse.

The identification of question asking can be organized around the
negotiation cycle of counseling transaction, information retrieval, and
content analyses. Counseling interactional analysis serves the purpose
of the individual who, because of a lack in his cognitive environment,
is unable to satisfactorily move from sense experience to interpreted
perception or concept. Interactional content analysis, consequently,
is a significant element in the stance of any communicator whose purpose is to identify specific patterns of response that contribute to the
purpose of the interview. In a sense, any counseling response to another's
unorganized experience is an inferential interpretation of behavior content whether expressed verbally or nonverbally.

The three specializations of media, library and information science
vary in the focus of their attention on the retrieval aspects of their services. The traditional concept of reference service has been as often
considered and practiced as a tutorial experience for the patron as it
has been the provision of retrieved data. Information science aims to
remove any burden on the patron; a machine search based upon a profile or individually formulated inquiry strategy delivers the pertinent
reference abstracts and/or documents to the patron. Media science
has been concerned with the patron's ability to effectively prepare and
deliver messages on the one hand, and on the other with individual access to mediated environments as, for example, in a learning laboratory.

FOUR

INDIVIDUAL NEGOTIATION

The previous two chapters have delineated the conditions within
which the intrapersonal development of the patron can commence. Following the behavioral cycle, the patron has been encouraged to articulate
his felt need by talking about the situation in which his concern or interest arose and continues to persist. As the "conversation" continues in
the counseling interview, the patron is induced to describe and analyze
the context of his situation with the view of identifying the constraints
and opportunities which may exist in it.

From the opportunity set, the patron selects his goal(s) and then,
in effect, ranks the constraints which appear to be keeping him from
reaching that goal. The constraints constitute the problem(s) which he
has to solve. Perhaps upon analysis and reflection, the patron may already have enough information to solve his problem. More than likely,
however, he will need additional information which will be retrieved from
the organized message space of the resource agency. In other instances,
referral will have to be made outside the agency to other community resources.

The steps in this procedure which stimulate the behavioral vector
within the patron are not new. In fact, they are but an application of
the general problem solving model. Nevertheless, an operational and
developmental model of the professional helping relationship which is
consistent with the social objectives of media, library, and information
science has not until recently been available. There are in the model
seventeen developmental steps in two phases: intrapersonal development
and interpersonal development.

The model has been explicated in considerable detail; the reader
is referred to Communication Science and Technology (104) for a more
extended treatment. The steps in the first phase, intrapersonal development, are listed below; the steps in the second phase are listed in the
following chapter:

Intrapersonal Development

Patron appears before the professional mediator indicating some interest. The professional catalyst conceives this contact to be one of a series and inquires whether the results of patron's previous contacts were satisfactory.

Patron is given an initial counseling interview in which information about his interests, life goals and ability to use information sources may be obtained.

In those instances where the patron is too inchoate to discuss deep-felt concerns, audiovisual therapy or browsing in thematic displays may need to be used before actually proceeding to the second step.

At this point, in order to understand the problem-solving model of communication, the patron may need some instruction in the use of library resources as a method of thinking.

Employing the general problem solving model, the mediating professional together with the patron proceed to enlarge the encounter to include outer-form materials which are more contextually oriented than subject classified.

When the subject and point of view have been established to the patron's initial satisfaction, a retrieval strategy based on a boolean or other logic is developed to search the descriptor file.

Document drops are examined in a "technical reading" for their information surprise value. If the information is not satisfactory to the patron, the search terms are regenerated and a new search strategy developed.

When a match has been achieved between the patron's goals and the kinds of information available, the professional mediator suggests related concepts and contexts in the exit interview for possible follow-up activity.

Patron enters upon a program of continuing development either in cognitive content mapping or in an n-dimensional matrix of interlocking situations and relationships.

Employing the method of case-load, the mediating professional is ready on a continuing basis to assist the patron to enter the communications system at any point and be expedited to any other point he may wish to travel.

Since many sources are available they have to be carefully matched to the goal to be achieved and to the task conditions for which they are to be employed. For example, pictures and motion may be substituted for concepts. Dialog and group discussion may enhance the intrapersonal communication skills of reading, viewing and listening.

The developmental steps in the intrapersonal phase of the behavioral cycle have been used to introduce this chapter in order to place in perspective the librarian's contribution to reading guidance or bibliotherapy as it is sometimes called. Reading guidance makes certain demands on the patron. Books and reading are presumed to be good for people; and if the patron will only participate with patience many of his concerns and interests will be met within the pages of the materials prescribed by the librarian.

Reading Guidance

Where reading guidance was practiced to best advantage, the initial librarian-patron interface grew out of any information provided by the patron. The discussion devolved around the patron's need for coming to the agency, any goals he may have in mind, and his previous background in the subject or topic. At this point, the traditional librarian would shunt the conversation into a display of his humanistic book knowledge in a sort of materials developmental pattern as exhibited in Table 3, Control of Patron-Librarian Interface.

The patron was moved from one part of the collection to another to a point where his interest lead him to browse more thoroughly. The conversational "lubricant" grew out of the librarian's broad knowledge of books:

> Effective reading guidance rests upon a strong foundation
> of the librarians knowing books, authors, publishers, and
> subject matter, judging accurately purpose and quality, and
> identifying correctly use and users. As many books as pos-
> sible should be read or examined carefully and the opinions
> of others sought. Equally important, is the knowledge and
> use of reviews and of reading guidance aids, reading lists,

Table 3

Control of Patron–Librarian Interface

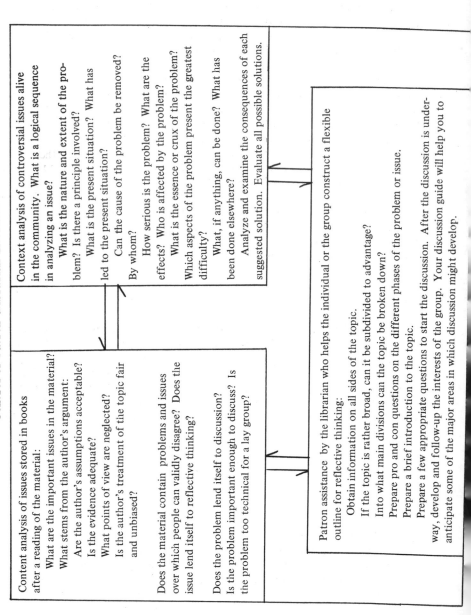

Content analysis of issues stored in books after a reading of the material:

What are the important issues in the material?

What stems from the author's argument:

Are the author's assumptions acceptable?

Is the evidence adequate?

What points of view are neglected?

Is the author's treatment of the topic fair and unbiased?

Does the material contain problems and issues over which people can validly disagree? Does the issue lend itself to reflective thinking?

Does the problem lend itself to discussion?

Is the problem important enough to discuss? Is the problem too technical for a lay group?

Context analysis of controversial issues alive in the community. What is a logical sequence in analyzing an issue?

What is the nature and extent of the problem? Is there a principle involved?

What is the present situation? What has led to the present situation?

Can the cause of the problem be removed? By whom?

How serious is the problem? What are the effects? Who is affected by the problem?

What is the essence or crux of the problem? Which aspects of the problem present the greatest difficulty?

What, if anything, can be done? What has been done elsewhere?

Analyze and examine the consequences of each suggested solution. Evaluate all possible solutions.

Patron assistance by the librarian who helps the individual or the group construct a flexible outline for reflective thinking:

Obtain information on all sides of the topic.

If the topic is rather broad, can it be subdivided to advantage?

Into what main divisions can the topic be broken down?

Prepare pro and con questions on the different phases of the problem or issue.

Prepare a brief introduction to the topic.

Prepare a few appropriate questions to start the discussion. After the discussion is underway, develop and follow-up the interests of the group. Your discussion guide will help you to anticipate some of the major areas in which discussion might develop.

and bibliographies by the specialist. The librarians
ability to advise individuals, to help them find and choose
what they need from books, and to develop lifetime reading
habits for learning and pleasure, depends on his ability to
read critically and widely (115).

Selection of materials was and continues to be a basic knowledge
and skill in the professional repertoire of every advisor. The same
principles which, unfortunately, are also used to build collections that
limit access are employed in selecting materials from that collection
for educational programming. Content evaluation questions include the
following:

Are the materials usable in direct relation to an advisory
guidance program? To a specific experience, or problem-
solving activity?

Is the content to be communicated by the material useful
and important? For the individual? For the community?
For society?

Will the material contribute to major self-instructional
purposes? And, toward the major goals of the patron?

Does the difficulty level of the intrapersonal communication program coincide with the understandings, abilities,
attitudes, and appreciations of the participants?

Will the material be likely to call for vicarious experiences,
thinking, reacting, discussing, studying?

Does the self-instructional program warrant use of a
variety of media? If so, what is the relation of the software (program) to hardware (equipment)?

Is the content to be communicated presented in terms of
problems and activities of the patron, such as the problem
solving approach? Logically arranged subject matter may
be called for at advanced levels of study, or like a tutorial
study outline.

Is the content to be presented by the material sufficient in
concepts and relationships to achieve the desired guidance
objective?

Does the material possess appropriate data content to
facilitate the process of inference? Does number of examples warrant sound conclusions? Accuracy and recency
of publication?

In advisory counseling, critical appraisal must continually be subject to evaluation of both the materials and the accompanying techniques.
There is no magic in, nor end to evaluation. It is a continuing process
that is built into the total intrapersonal experience. The following questions may be extended as the communicator gains insight in introducing
material at the appropriate "teachable moment."

What did participants like about the content of the material
used?

Did participants react to the content the way expected?

Was the material too trivial or superficial for the characteristics of the group?

Was the material actually worth the time and effort, or
should other types of material have been located?

Did the content of the materials help to release the
energies of the participants?

Was irrelevant material used? Can it be eliminated?

Media materials and services may be used for two different but
closely related purposes: motivating people to participate in informational
and educational experiences and motivating them to learn. Almost identical principles of guidance are used in either instance. In motivating
to participate, resources are so orchestrated around an issue that it
becomes difficult for the individual to avoid thinking about the message.
No one ever stops learning. To move beyond participation and motivate
individuals to learn they must be involved in sequential experiences
where learning can occur.

Conceptual interlock is at the core of the patron-intrapersonal-
resource relationship. Instructed in the use of one piece of media, one
reserve book, or in one library service routine, subsequent utilization
of that equipment, book or routine will in turn give further and related
instruction. In this manner, the patron is introduced to the process of
search and discovery of knowledge in available learning resources.
The requirements for information surprises call for the immediate avail-

ability for use singly or in combination of the full range of communication resources.

Increased participation in and understanding of information sources are expected as citizens follow up more of the increased perceptual stimuli to which they are exposed through mass media programming along insights of their own choosing. Involvement is fundamental to the communications process. Citizens should find available many community and library experiences contrived for learning which they can follow-up on their own. The guidance counselor can show by his patient attitude that the patron is not a nuisance; that he is willing to listen to the whole problem; that the patron's request is of concern and importance to him.

The librarian should show equal consideration to all patrons and be sensitive to all requests. He should never be rude, brusk, or unkind to any seeker of light diversion or simple answers, while expending full energies for the intellectually inclined seeker. The guidelines for such service have been summarized in a set of prescriptions (115):

Introduce and maintain a friendly, constructive approach to the patron's concern or interest. The librarian's questions should grow out of what the patron has said.

Patron's comments, his problem, and the way he presents them are clues to his level of knowledge on the subject, the point-of-view with which he approaches it, the ways he expects to use the material he wants, any special abilities or limitations in relation to its study, his degree of enthusiasm or earnest purpose.

Encourage the reader to make the problem clear, but help him in keeping it free from embarrassment for himself.

Never give advice on the solution of personal problems, but provide the sources of advice.

Keep the interview constantly moving toward the goal, such as some aspect of growth for the reader during the interview.

Refocus the too-ambitious planner; stimulate the indifferent to a plan worthy of the reader's capacity.

Let the steps to be taken evolve in consultation with the reader, not presented as an unalterable prescription by the librarian.

Relate the length of the interview to the need and to the continuing favorable interview conditions.

Interpret the proposed materials to the reader so that he
may make the best use of them.

Strike a happy balance between making the reader dependent
upon the librarian and making him feel that henceforth he is
on his own completely.

A librarian may be prone to devote more time and to give specialized
treatment to the more difficult questions, based on his own standards
and ethical views of professional performance. He is prepared to go
further in pursuing informational requests which pose a challenge to his
intellect and abilities as being on a high level of sophistication and therefore more worthy of his efforts. He will perhaps determine the relative
importance of an inquirer's need based upon his assessment of the pres-
tige, the authority, the personality and appearance, or the presumed
social, economic, or intellectual group which the patron represents.
"Despite the democratic ethic upon which library service is founded, the
human tendency to choose to deal with individuals or situations which do
not threaten, or to cater to those presumed to be most important, remains unbridled" (21).

The librarian who appears to be less competent because he ponders
longer, questions more, or asks for more time to consider the problem
will often provide the more valuable service by turning up better sources
of information. One of the advantages of the human brain over a computer is its ability to work quite well with the vague ideas that any computer would reject as formless. Another human advantage is the ability
to interpret the facial expressions and gestures that provide the feedback in any interpersonal communication. The librarian will be informed
as to how well his messages are being received and interpreted by the
smiles, frowns, shrugs, or general shifting and squirming that his
patrons unconsciously send back to him.

SUBJECT CONTENT NEGOTIATION

The general pattern of advisory guidance has been summarized in
a number of components. The system as presented in the following components may be considered as a general model within which each patron
will negotiate his inquiry (115):

The librarian asks for details on the problem by asking a broad opening question. The librarian interrupts the reader's explanation only to ask questions that clarify his understanding of the problem. During the first part of the interview the librarian will be deciding which of the three major services will provide the best kind of help, and decides the best initial step to propose to the reader.

The librarian checks his understanding of the problem with the reader. He may use different key terms so that if the reader's vocabulary was open to misunderstanding, that can be clarified immediately.

When the problem seems clarified, the librarian will propose a way of going about providing help, and will discuss it with the reader: a reading list, a group of books to borrow immediately, checking a directory of social agencies for possible help, etc. The long range plan for solving the problem may involve all three types of services: materials, non-materials resources, referrals.

Take the first step of the plan with the reader before the conclusion of the interview, and make clear any kind of continuing cooperation he may expect from the librarian. The first step may be a reading list prepared on the spot; or a beginning book to read as preliminary to a list; or an introduction to a specialist (the children's librarian, perhaps); or a telephone call to an agency to arrange an interview; or writing down the address of the museum that has the information he needs.

The follow-up work may consist only of recording the interview, if the problem is now out of the hands of the librarian; or it may mean the preparation of an annotated list of books or films; or it may mean gathering of information about community resources that will both serve this reader and provide a backlog of knowledge for the next such request.

In some cases, the advisor can raise some issues which will force the patron to think about other points of view, or perhaps to revise his value system. This revision of value systems should not be attempted too often unless the patron shows some desire to learn how others think. Certainly the advisor will not be able to provide a better system

of values than the patron originally held. The advisor's duty is only to
present materials covering all points of view on the issue, and challenge
the patron to consider new viewpoints, not to change the patron's beliefs.
In any event, value change is accomplished, if it is achieved at all, through
an "objective" method:

Searching for information:

Analyze the subject: specific or general; part of what
larger subject; related to what other subjects?

Consult card catalog and note the books or classifications
which may be useful (shelf-list may be used as substitute
for card catalog).

Check shelves for possible sources — examine book's
index; table of contents, illustrations, etc.; appendices;
bibliographies.

Systematic searching:

newest to oldest

use cumulated indexes

possible variations in spelling and filing

give complete bibliographical data in listing or citing
references.

Seeking assistance from the librarian:

To clarify problem or suggest method of searching.

Self-reliance should be encouraged, but staff time
should be used wisely.

Contacts outside the library should be made by librarian
or with the specific knowledge and approval of the librarian.

Securing information from sources outside the library:

What person nearby has information?

Is there an office close by with information; a laboratory;
a museum?

What other libraries could help:

State Library and/or Bibliographic Center

Special subject collection in the state

Interlibrary loan courtesies:

Give complete identification of the book desired;
or explain briefly how the subject material requested is to be used. "Interlibrary loans" may
be restricted to use in the library. Keep careful track of borrowed material, date due, etc.

Advisory guidance provides an individualized method whereby a
patron may be helped in the behavioral cycle task of problem description,
the identification of constraints and opportunities, and the reference retrieval of exploratory data. Making contact with patrons who will want
to ask for help is largely a matter of creating situations within which
interpersonal communication can occur. In fact, professional communications should be at the point of contact when patrons enter the media,
library, and information center.

In traditional librarianship, which did not consciously and deliberately
employ advisory guidance in the behavior change process, the interface,
if it ever did develop, usually grew out of a patron's demand for a good
book to read. Since the demand could not be met directly, the librarian
countered with questions of his own:

Have you read (seen) anything recently that you liked?

Do you want something giving more or better coverage of the
same topic, or with the same mood?

Perhaps you would like to deepen your knowledge in that
particular area?

An urbane and literate conversation combined with a walking display
of book "riches" on the shelves has always been considered to be the
ideal way for the librarian to develop a close rapport with the patron.

The more literate and interesting the librarian's conversation could be made, the less painless would be the process of information getting on the part of the patron. For the few sophisticated readers who could appreciate such a service, book advisory conversations were a pleasant and cultivated experience. Indeed, the highlight in any patron's contact with a humanistic librarian was to receive an individualized reading list specially prepared around his unique concerns and interests.

Fortunate indeed were those patrons whose specially prepared reading list was also annotated. The purpose of this living "bouquet" was to describe each book's contents, point out interesting tidbits and appraise the material for the reader. Of course, an effort was made to be objective and point out facts pertinent to the reader's purpose. But the real "message" which came over to most readers was the fact that the annotation was a major method of communicating to others the librarian's knowledge of the book. The wider and deeper that knowledge, the more perceptive and critical the annotation would be.

Over time, the annotated reading list was expanded into the reading course or program of carefully chosen selections to meet the purpose, need, and ability of the individual reader. It had purpose and direction and was primarily designed to bring the patron into sequential contact with a librarian. The relationship was a tutorial and advisory one in which the reader's reactions were discussed from time to time. Steps in preparing a reading course include the following (115):

Note possible titles, bibliographical information, other opinions and reviews. The search for suggestions includes the library catalog, special annotated catalogs, basic selection and reading guidance aids, existing book lists and subject bibliographies.

Assemble books and articles for reading and examination. Criticisms and reviews are checked and a specialist may be consulted. Only a part of a book or article may suffice. Each reading is evaluated by the usual selection criteria of authority, purpose, content, form, reading level and style.

Make a final selection with specific readers in mind (not one's own biases and preferences) and arrange the readings in a logical order according to purpose and use: chronological, alphabetical, subject catagories.

Write annotations which will appeal to readers. Describe the subject matter; evaluate and relate readings to each other. It is well to give some idea of the complexity of treatment, the reading level, and quality of material.

Print the final list in as attractive a format as possible with careful attention to proofreading, design and layout. The more attractive the appearance, the greater will be reader appeal.

Eventually it became fashionable for librarians to do group work. The book talk, the story hour and a variety of games became popular. In addition to the necessary public speaking and activity skills, the art and function of the annotation remained a constant skill. The purpose of the group presentation was still to describe and appraise the contents of books for potential readers. The manner of presentation was admittedly dramatic or subjective but thereby became more interesting and stimulating. The audience was baited by the selection of an incident which would titillate and motivate a potential reader to actually read.

The discussion group process has been exploited by librarians as a key through which the individual can be reached and stimulated to undertake reading programs. In the American Heritage Project, librarians were taught how to expand their reader conversations into a discussion method adopted to the context of group activity. The content of the group enterprise, that which served as an agenda, grew out of the art of the annotation. Reading course design served as the basic model upon which many book discussion groups and film forums were designed.

When it came to instruction in the use of organized message and index space, the librarians have been less successful with the group process. Instruction has been largely a tutorial affair where on a one-to-one basis it is relatively easy to get away with intuitive teaching. It remains a fact of the matter that librarians do not know how to create the conditions within which teachable moments can occur in a group. Lacking the self-discipline of the classroom, group instruction in library use turns out more often than not to be a grand tour of the facility.

ENCOUNTER SYSTEM

The librarian must accept each question as it is presented and then classify the question in terms of purpose, i.e., determine the topic and its aspect. The patron may feel that since he has presented his request,

his part of the interaction is finished and that it is now the librarian's
responsibility to provide the information. Often the patron does not
realize the extent of the materials available on the requested subject.
He may believe that the librarian can give him all pertinent information
and that the information provided will automatically and completely
cover his needs. He may not realize that if the librarian gives him all
the available information, it might take him hours to wade through all
of it. On the other hand, if the librarian presents only a part of the
available information, the patron may not get a large part of the information he needs.

The patron should be helped to realize that the librarian can do a
much more efficient job of presenting the necessary materials if he knows
specifically what the patron has in mind rather than a vague, general
area in which to search.   The librarian can often limit the field of search
by restating the patron's request, or by asking such questions as: "What
is it you need to find out about . . . ?"; or "Let me be sure. You are
looking for. . . ?" Sometimes it is even helpful to use the process of
elimination: "Am I right in thinking that you don't want anything on . . . ?"
The tone of voice, the honest attitude and appearance of wanting to help
will often make such questions easier for the patron to accept.

The question must also be defined in terms of scope. The scope
will depend upon the need of the patron and the difficulty of the question.
A student who is doing a report on the Grand Canyon may be satisfied
with an encyclopedia article; whereas the student whose parents are
planning a trip to the West will want several books and magazine articles
that provide more depth and detail about getting there, staying there,
and the surrounding points of interest.

The patron's needs will determine the point of view and what form
of materials the librarian will retrieve. From the interview, the librarian must determine how much time the patron is willing to spend,
how much reading he is prepared to do, and how well and on what level
he will be able to interpret and use the results of the librarian's search.
These factors will usually depend to some extent on age, education, interest, experience, and the capabilities of the patron.

The librarian who tries to hurry the patron by guessing at his problem before it has been fully explained, or by jumping to conclusions
and providing materials that are not what the patron wants, is doing a
disservice. The patron may feel rushed or that his time is being
wasted. Searching without a definite objective is purposeless waste of
time. Wasting the patron's time destroys his confidence in the professionalism of the librarian.

The librarian cannot assume a professional role unless he merits the patron's acceptance of him in the role of expert. The patron will not consider the librarian as an expert unless he exhibits a purposeful and assured attitude together with the ability to handle requests efficiently and provide the needed materials without a great deal of wasted energy. This does not mean that the librarian should be expected to show a computer-like speed when dealing with his patrons. Often the librarian who presents materials immediately does not offer the best sources available.

The system employed by the professional catalyst is flexible and dynamic. It is cybernetic, involving the patron at point of contact and at any point in time. Through a series of feedback loops, the patron can move to any other point in the system at any point in time. The aim is to assist the patron in achieving maturity in listening, viewing and reading through involvement with a wide range of developmental and encounter materials. The major components of the system are displayed in Figure 3, Encounter System.

The materials encounter skills of listening, viewing and reading are taught to patrons by means of tutorial techniques largely in advisory counseling situations. The learnings are induced in individualized contexts by means of what might be called activity therapy and advisory sessions. Fargo (37), in her activity books, established a pattern which has become fairly standard with children. On the other hand, Flexner (40) pioneered a materials advisory service which has become the accepted procedure of working with adults. In more recent years, these approaches have been augmented by media and museum specialists through a wide range of materials production skills for children, youth and adults.

Such a self-tutorial program is based upon the context analysis of the counseling and developmental interview and anticipates the more rigorous analysis of content as found in reference retrieval. Context analysis is an aspect of audience research where the "receiver" is an individual patron. The content analysis is a form of document appraisal where the intentions or purposes of one or more senders (authors) are identified and mapped into patterns ("reading" lists). These patterns comprise a subject area as presented by one or more authors, film producers or recording artists. Aspects of the subject and related topics as well as variant points of view are included on the self-tutorial list which is presumed to be a mapped pattern within which the patron's "real" concern is embedded.

It must, of course, be realized that the mapping can never be an accurate point for point isomorphy. The congruence between the inten-

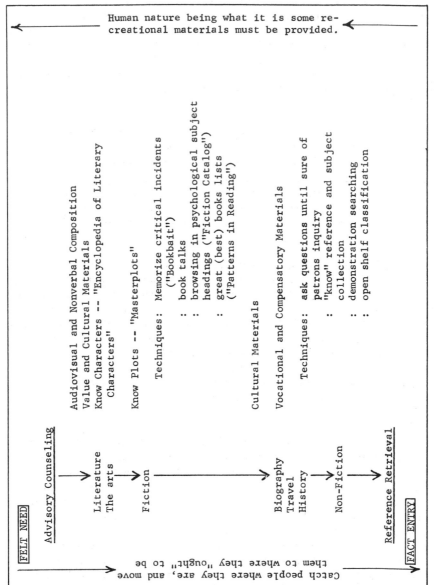

Figure 3 . Encounter System

tion set of the senders and the intentions and purposes of the audience
or of one patron is never complete. The degree of congruence varies
directly with the competence of the communicator both in analyzing the
context of a patron's concern or interest and in making content analyses
of one or more documents as well as with his professional skill in
matching these two inferences about purpose and viewpoints, the subject
and its aspects. In any event, the self-tutorial document list as a product of the analyses and inferences is, in effect, negotiated by the patron
reacting to the catalytic suggestions of the communicator (Figure 4).

In daily work the advisor is problem-oriented rather than disci-
pline-oriented. He becomes aware, as the guidance process develops,
of a need that can be met through the application of information and educational problem solving. Problem solving is an iterative process which
starts with an estimate and continues with successively more sophisticated
solutions until the results required are obtained. Problem-solving demands a variety of solution-trials and methods and the application of
greater accuracy than may thought at first to be necessary. The guidance interface is located within the steps of the general problem solving
model:

Problem definition is the most important step and often the
most difficult. This step includes initial investigation and
considerable data gathering. In the process, the initial
general and vague consideration of the problem becomes
specific and concrete.

Assumption listing could be considered as a part of the
first step, because the assumptions are important for defining the problem. The assumptions are usually listed
because the solution cannot be expected to apply to situations beyond the original assumptions.

Consider available solutions and methods and select one
or more. Solutions are not limited to analytical or mathe-
matical ones. The library collection may reveal a solution
in a document.

Solve by experimenting and try several methods to see which
is going to work out best. Creative brain-storming may help.
In fact, most problems are solved by a combination of methods,
and often by techniques not developed or readily available.

Check carefully, especially the effect of assumptions on the
solution and vice versa. The entire problem definition and
assumptions should be examined in relation to solution results
for consistency and reasonableness.

Situation	Recommendation (Individual or group Program)	Reason (Objective)
Some people have just taken a basic course in bridge. They wish to continue meeting to improve their practice.		
Several people want to know more about world affairs.		
More than fifteen young people would like to have help in preparing for marriage.		
A labor representative wants to help his union members gain an understanding of a new piece of legislation and make a decision as to what they should do about it.		
Two civic leaders seek your advice about the rising racial tension in the community.		
A group of recent high school graduates comes to you to ask for a room in which to meet once a week to continue friendships.		
A group of retired couples has organized for fellowship and education. What processes should they follow in planning a year's program of monthly meetings. List sample events.		

Figure 4. Planning Educational Experiences

Generalize and extend results. Solutions to one specific
problem may point the way to an entirely different approach
or design. At the very least, it is usually possible to generalize for a class of problems so that the same work does
not have to be done over again.

Context analysis of the patron's life situation has been developed
in the previous chapter on developmental counseling and interviewing.
On the other hand, advisory counseling traditionally known as "readers"
advisory or bibliotherapy, builds upon context analysis and anticipates
the foundation of content and subject analysis upon which reference retrieval and eventually information retrieval rest. Shores (130) has provided a schema for the design of self-tutorials which leads directly into
the reference retrievals considered in the next chapter:

Prepare topical outline of subject, its aspects and variant
viewpoints.

> Sources: Dewey, Library of Congress and other
> classifications; introductory textbook;
> encyclopedia article; descriptor thesau-
> rus; relative index.

Make a list of the important terms; look up definitions and
synonym set.

> Sources: General dictionary; subject dictionary;
> general thesaurus.

Decide on the half-dozen or so most important names of
persons, two or three significant learned societies and
professional associations, and the leading periodicals of
the field.

> Sources: Encyclopedia article; textbook; Ulrich's
> Periodicals Directory; citation indexes
> and abstracts.

Get acquainted generally with kinds of data or processes
important to the subject.

> Sources: Handbooks; manuals; formularies; data
> banks.

Find out whether government agencies are concerned with subject and if there are audio-visual materials.

Sources: Document indexes; audiovisual bibilogra-
phies; mediagraphic control.

Locate and read a popular introduction to the subject.

Sources: Standard Catalog series or other selected
lists and self-tutorial aids.

Indicate three or four pressing problems, trends and social imperatives.

Sources: Yearbooks; periodicals; newspapers; annual
abstracts and guides.

The self-tutorial of reading, viewing and listening experiences is designed to help expedite two accomplishments or behavioral outcomes by the patron: move his level of articulation of a life situation together with its embedded concern or interest into further description and analysis which remains congruent with his affective domain; abstract the embedded concern or interest into a well formulated statement which can be sub-ject analyzed into a negotiable inquiry containing a subject or topic, its aspects and point of view.   These objectives are realized in dynamic and developmental negotiations and not in the step by step sequence of a linear array, however useful the latter may be for instructional pur-poses.

TUTORIAL INSTRUCTION

In achieving his objective, the patron may need further advisory counseling of the type traditionally known as instruction in "library" use.   Actually the patron more accurately learns the technique of in-formation "research" rather than the layout of an agency's building. The purpose of individual or group instruction in information search is to help the patron develop the following skills:

Identify the data needed which is pertinent or has surprise value for a given concern or interest.

Decide on the types of resource materials required on the basis of topic, aspect and form.

Learn to use the indexes and catalogs for lookup retrievals
of appropriate resources whether on the premises or out in
the community.

Learn to browse at the document file for a topic, its aspects
and form divisions in order to choose documents which may
contain sought-for data.

Select proper terms with which to search the index of a
document and find "pages" on which information surprise
may be found.

Skim the material for adequacy and relevance to the problem
context.

Read, view or listen in order to take adequate notes; organize
information and reach conclusions.

Make a bibliography of materials cited and sources used.

Eventually, perhaps as a result of experience and repetition
in using the above search pattern, learn to browse in the subject file in order to correlate coordinate terms and the regressive
relation between descriptor set and class mark.

The resource specialist helps the patron not only to identify his
inquiry, but also to formulate it in the language which has been used by
the communications' enterprise to record, publish and control knowledge. Variables in the information retrieval enterprise include the
following: 1) ways in which authors have written about the concepts,
ideas or subjects of interest to the inquirer; 2) how, when and where
the publishing industry has placed authors' works in the public domain;
3) ways in which librarians, documentalists and information scientists
have analyzed and controlled the record of these works.

A search protocol has to be outlined and the terms structured into
a logical format so that matching terms will cause appropriate document
representations to drop from the file. The objective of an information
retrieval method is, "To provide on demand, with maximum usefulness
and precision and at minimum expense, pertinent information in response
to any reasonable question being defined as any serious question of obvious or potential significance, posed by a person who has a socially important reason for desiring the answer to the question (77)." The following
points indicate the major steps in the search strategy:

Questions or problem must exist and be recognized and it
must be verbalized or recorded for communication to the
librarian in a searching activity.

Question must be analyzed by the librarian in order to
provide clues that will be useful in formulating a search
stragegy and interview abstract.

Terms in the interview abstract must be translated into the
terminology and into a logical pattern conforming to the systems analysis and storage of records in the file.

Clue terms in the search strategy must be selected and
formalized in a language and a program conforming to the
requirements of the method used for searching.

Searching machinery must be set in action so that a response
may be obtained.

The resource specialist must not only be sensitive to the needs of
the user but also skilled in the complexities of message space which
organizes the overwhelming totality of authors who have ever written.
Part of the difficulty experienced by the user is due to an unfamiliarity
with the code of organization which has been developed to meet the needs
of most users: classification, bibliographic entry and subject abstracting.

In addition to the difficulty over organizational patterns, considerable
confusion arises out of the user's lack of precision in thinking. Unfamiliarity with the terminology of subject headings causes readers to phrase
inquiries in general and comprehensive terms. The user focused upon
specific objectives has less difficulty than the unfocused reader in determining the author's purposes in writing. Further difficulty occurs because the reader views his inquiry from his own self-interest, his individual preoccupation and motivation which may be contrary to the author's
purpose in writing materials.

In almost every instance, the field of search must be narrowed
down through a dialog-interview, step by step, until the appropriate subject heading or index term is agreed upon. Then the search of the bibliographic apparatus may be successful. The dialog or interview with
the reader is essential to help him clarify his previous thinking about
the topic of inquiry as well as the new dimensions raised in the presence
of a highly organized and complex collection of materials — the visible

embodiment of knowledge. A knowledge and appreciation of the card catalog, subject bibliography and indexing is particularly valuable to the user, especially in using the cryptic language of bibliographic and subject entry.

FIVE

GROUP NEGOTIATION

While the study of individual behavior is important, it becomes increasingly significant when the individual enters into the interactive environment of the group adaptive control organism. The group process is a cybernetic system encompassing participant intentions and behavioral outcomes in dynamic disequilibrium. A collection of individuals is not necessarily a group. It is only when they become an interactive adaptive control organism with a definable membership and group consciousness that a sense of shared purpose develops. Participants communicate with and influence one another in order to accomplish the purposes for which they joined the group.

There are many roles which people play in the life stream of any community and for which they may need information. These roles are related to the social values and ethics of the communal entity as well as the individual's perceived self-relation to that society. The roles people play are in response to the social rules which maintain that society and which become dramatized and individualistic versions of the mores.

The rules of the social game are sometimes referred to as etiquette, a polite version of the deeply imbedded socialization which has taken place in the individual. Communicative activity in a group situation heightens the necessity of viable information as well as places an imperative upon each participant to supply it effectively. Each member of the group is constantly engaged in dealing with two kinds of problems:

Efforts to achieve his conscious purpose for being there — learning to appreciate literature, become a more knowledgeable citizen, sharpen his thinking.

Efforts to resolve his hidden problems of adapting to other people, of anxiety about what other members think of him, and subduing inclinations towards flight.

Because of these needs, small group work is considered here as an extension of counseling and guidance in media, library and information

centers. As much as the resource specialist may hate to admit it, there
is a symbiotic relationship between service to the individual and small
group counseling and guidance. In those instances where service to the
individual excludes group considerations, the individual being served
is "short changed"; and he may abort his developing social behaviors.

Counseling and guidance cannot be practiced in a social vacuum as
if the only purpose were to relate people to knowledge. The objective
is not so much to relate people to books as it is to relate materials to
people, or rather data which can have some surprise value for human
beings. It is the human being who must be nurtured within the communicative contexts or conditions to which information is being applied. In
other words, the information has to become kinetic in the real life behaviors of people.

The purpose of this chapter is not to explicate group counseling;
that is done in a companion volume to this one, Group Dynamics and
Individual Development (108). The objective here is to point out the relationship which exists between group counseling and guidance and that
of individual advisory and retrieval services. The questioning process
which is absolutely essential in the group process will build competencies
in the resource specialist that will help him improve not only interpersonal skills but also his interviewing methods.

A systems approach should be taken to the real life problems of the
individual. Real life solutions to his problems cannot be found in books
and reading — simply some information which the individual will have
to learn to apply, if not with help, then despite the librarian's traditional
guidance. In group counseling, the professional change agent is involved
with a number of participants who may be at various levels of ability
to gather information and apply it to the context in which they are involved. At one level, the focus of attention is upon the attitudes and
emotions, the choices and values involved in interpersonal relationships;
and the resource specialist must be prepared to deal with these considerations (108).

At another level, the communicator operates as a resource consultant, counseling and guiding one or more of the participants in retrieving
and applying relevant information at significant moments. The overall
objectives to be achieved in individual and group counseling are frequently similar. The resource specialist, as a service rendering member of the small group, uses his counseling methods to get the behavioral
cycle of the group going. His guidance methods are employed to help the
participants individually and as a group advance towards their goals.

DEVELOPMENTAL SYSTEM

The rationale for a systems approach to the communicative activity of the resource specialist in media, library, and information science has been developed elsewhere (104). The conditions within which communicative activity can occur have been delineated in a set of developmental steps or tasks. These tasks are developmental in human terms as the patron is nurtured in his ability not only to retrieve information but also to apply it in real life contexts which are frequently of a transactional nature.

The first phase of these developmental steps was considered in the previous chapter. The intrapersonal tasks of the patron are met by the resource specialist, if need be, before the patron is encouraged to participate in group experiences. On the other hand, the patron cannot be limited to these tasks alone but should be motivated to participate in small group activity. The steps in the interpersonal phase of the patron's social development include the following (104):

Interpersonal Development

Patron engages in a variety of communications situations and attains successive but individual levels of competence. At each level or departure point, the librarian employing interviewing or discussion skills helps the patron access his own level of development.

If the patron requires more support in this assessment, at any level, than can be given by the agency professional, referral is made and contact established with a helping consultant, an accepting group, or responsive community movement.

Periodically, the patron is encouraged to join with other persons in teams, seminars, or groups for the purpose of developing new ideas or creating new programs. The most important criterion for joining such groups is the prior attainment of suitable skills or knowledge relevant to the activity to be undertaken and the processes of the group. Counseling for group processes is as essential as for content.

As the patron develops into a resource person in his own right, the professional communicator offers him the opportunity of conducting sessions in the library's own programs of communications. Supportive counseling sessions as well as rehearsal demonstrations before and after these leadership situations may be needed.

Periodically, the patron should have the opportunity of taking responsibility for the development and conducting of entire programs whether on the media center premises, over closed circuit television or through the channels of mass media owned by the network of media, library and information centers.

Eventually, when the patron had developed his ability as one of the communications "elite" he may be able to take leadership in community development and movements.

These tasks are general accomplishments presumably common for all citizens and would need to be individualized in specific instances. However, a display of these ultimate objectives may present a system which will yield specific instructional goals and learning outcomes desirable to a wide range of patrons. Intrapersonal development is nurtured by individual services such as counseling, guidance and retrieval; whereas interpersonal development is engendered in interactive small group processes. Once nurtured, the individual together with his librarian guide may be in a position to venture into the larger context of community endeavor (105).

Obviously, these developmental tasks cannot be practised by the patron in an interpersonal vacuum, and even less so in a media library or information center regardless of its comprehensive and well organized collections. Materials are not sufficient for communication. The information gleaned has to be applied in an interpersonal and even community context. The small group offers opportunities for involvement possibly not available anywhere else. In fact, the small group, not books and reading is the milieu for applications of service to the individual.

The small group is an information processing system where the individual can observe, if he inputs it, the effect of the information which surprised him. Otherwise, the information will probably decompose in his own mind and will probably serve no other useful purpose. The small group is a particularly valuable experience for the resource specialist to have. It is seldom that the typical librarian sees much if any effect of the vast amounts of data supplied every day to patrons; but in the small group he has immediate feedback with at least a few individuals.

Group dynamics operates to maximize the number of stimuli to which each participant pays attention in the group context. The function of the group experience is to increase the range of surpriseful stimuli based

on relevance and usability. In general terms, information surprise is
generated by the participants themselves within the group interaction.
Basically, the group is a constructive force, a manifestation of the capacity for mutual aid among individuals. The participants not only receive aid and learn to help others but more importantly they receive feedback on their role as information suppliers and thinkers in the group.

The group process is a unique learning experience because all participants can be involved in both the teaching and the learning enterprise.
Learning goes on all the time; it is impossible to be alive and awake in
a group and not respond to the multitude of stimuli being generated by
the group's activity. Although the group is not the only situation in which
learning can and does occur, it is unique in one very important respect.
In the formal classroom lecture situation the individual can only act for
and within himself about the information he is receiving. But in a group,
learner becomes teacher and teacher, learner. There is not only input
and then reaction, there is further input and further reaction.

Observations and ideas are tested out, and as they are accepted or
rejected and questioned or analyzed by the group, a learning-teaching
interactive process has been called into play. Even if a member makes
an observation or shares an insight and is met with silence, this too is
a reaction to which he must react. In a mature, flourishing group there
is a comfortable flow in this movement between learning and teaching.
The teaching mode does not make one a superauthority, nor does the
learning mode make one a less valued group member. It is perhaps the
role of the leader to support both these enterprises and to give both
processes their rightful place in the group.

The culture of a group is composed of its values, beliefs and goals.
The acceptance of the group's culture on the part of a participant is often
equivalent to a change in culture for him and thus is basically a reed-
ucational process. For an individual to accept a new system of values
and beliefs he must come to value his membership in the new group.
In other words, the group becomes more effective as an instrument for
his own behavioral change, than the retrieval work of a resource specialist can ever be.

Since the individual shares his educational aims with other members
of the group, it is useful to think of the individual in the group as having
needs for certain kinds of behavior necessary to accomplish group work.
For example, each member of the group needs to understand what other
members are saying. All members expect to have an opportunity to

challenge or to help develop an idea. All members expect that persons who continually impede effective thinking will be dealt with and that a climate will be created which will permit them to participate.

In this view of participation, then, one can think of any individual contribution to the discussion as satisfying one of two different kinds of needs. Both individual and group needs are met by some action of an individual. Such actions are roles which people play in a group.

An individual, emotional need of one of the members may, for example, be to gain status, or to find security by dominating.

A group need for accomplishing the work necessary to reach a common goal may, for example, be the harmonizing of different points of view or the clarification of a confusing situation.

In any group one can expect to find a number of different roles being played. Some of them coincide with the group's need to get the job done, and therefore help the discussion. Other roles serve individual needs which may or may not coincide with the group need; or they may tend to hinder the discussion. Consequently the reader is referred to the publication, Group Dynamics and Individual Development (108). A number of encounter simulations are included which constitute a base for a liberal education in group activity.

Service to small groups can be considered in relation to the various ways the resource specialist endeavors to meet the concerns and interests of participants. The professional communicator could, as one approach, proceed on an expressed, cognitive level which is typical of the Great Books and American Heritage projects. In this regard, Powell's basic work, Education for Maturity (113), still stands as a primary guide for such endeavors. On the other hand, group communicative programs are particularly suitable for adult concerns and interests. Group participation engenders a maturity of style and ability in order to think and work with other citizens.

People tend to develop behaviors which meet their needs and then cling to them, whether they make other people unhappy or not and whether they get in the way of constructive work or not. But the individual has a second purpose: his identified purpose of learning more about some subject, increasing his ability to think, improving himself in some way. These two purposes may complement each other but they may also come in conflict; satisfying some emotional need may interfere with the achievement of a self-educational aim.

Group dynamics is a process specifically useful to specialists in the
media, library, and information profession to bring about a sensitivity
to group process and individual behavior. The following learnings become internalized and constitute a base upon which the socialized individual can build further growth in other situations:

Learning how to learn from feedback. Each individual learns
to observe, and analyze his feelings, attitudes and those of
his fellows, as well as his interchanges with other members
of the group.

Learning how to give help as a corollary of the preceeding
objective. In learning how to learn, one also learns how
to give help, give feedback, extend oneself to others.

Developing effective membership involves the ability to create
a climate of trust and confidence. As individuals learn to observe and analyze their own and other participants' reactions,
the desired atmosphere for further learning is built.

ASSEMBLING THE POTENTIAL

A group can assemble and continue in existence for a number of
reasons. These reasons may include any or all of the following needs
as well as others: to identify with others working on a similar problem;
to define reality by testing how many participants need to see something
the same way for it to become real; to experience the learning involved
in a leadership role. After some initial success has been met by the
group, it may become self-satisfied or complacent. There is a considerable tendency towards a comfort level and the group may linger in
this "honeymoon" period.

Inevitably, one or more members will challenge the group with the
fact that it is on dead center. The group may then polarize about those
who want to maintain the comfort level as opposed to those who begin
to rock the boat. There is a polarity between the functions of group
maintenance and member self-maintenance. Once, however, the whole
group has worked out some compromise on this issue, group demands
will be regarded decreasingly as threats to individual rights. In recog-
nizing that compromises have succeeded, individuals become more trusting
of one another and feel less fearful of group pressures.

Although each individual participant may be different from the others, all of them have something in common. There is a common desire to learn, an interest in the same subject, a preference for learning with others rather than by themselves as is evident when a group of agency staff and neighborhood leaders come together to discuss the role of an agency in community affairs.

Every group is organized around some specific content. The group also has a learning and communications goal which involves that content. If the group is really working toward its accepted goal, then everything it does has some relevance to the content. One way is to think about the group as within a particular field of content which provides a focus for its effort. To the extent that subject matter makes different demands on the group, it is an important determinant of the effectiveness of the group effort.

Practically nothing in terms of content consequence is achieved during the first session of a group activity. Participants are much too busy studying the people around them, measuring themselves against those others, deciding how they like the communicator, and trying in general to become comfortable in the new surroundings.

The communicator must, from the outset, help to create a people's climate which will permit individual members of the group to assert their individuality and to realize that they are expected to participate. Members of the group must receive assurance and security (as well as common understandings and purposes) through a sharing in and understanding of the goals and limits of the program. The procedure to be used in achieving these goals must also be given sufficient consideration.

Taken together, the components of climate, leader, and content make up the major aspects of the group encounter situation. It is of fundamental importance that a climate be created within which communication can occur, such as the common study and analysis of agency-community concerns and interests. Since the communicator operates on the principle of accepting people where they are, at any education or interest level, his organized group activity may grow out of "bull sessions" or the initial enjoyment of conversation or discussion for its own sake.

The function of the initial leader is to transfer as rapidly as possible leadership to various participants. In the very beginning, with a new group, the leader will stimulate participation by bringing out as many members as possible. The following methods include the kinds of questions and the manner of statement which are designed to aid the most reluctant member in making a contribution:

> Ask questions which do not tend to put people on the spot by checking the amount or type of information that they have on a particular point. Questions which put people on the spot will draw out only the members of the group who have a store of facts and information and will inhibit the others.

> Use questions which do not merely call for a "yes or no" or "agree or disagree" answer. "Yes or no" questions do not stimulate discussion and merely set a pattern whereby members of the group feel that their role is one of being led, or misled, by a leader.

> Ask questions which are simple, clear and concise rather than wide open so that members of the group know what will lead to effective discussion. This will avoid confusion and will stimulate general participation.

The leader who has control over his own behavior determines the participation of the group. The leader is responsible for seeing that participation is measured not only in terms of the number participating but also in terms of the quality of participation. The leader's responsibility is not only one of permitting members to participate but also of ensuring that participation leads to thinking, learning and the sound development of ideas. A highly demanding style may stimulate attention but it also develops tensions and arguments. A highly permissive style may stimulate wide participation and a feeling of ease but it also results in more relaxed and less intense participation.

In the beginning, participation may well be stimulated by the leader, primarily to ensure that group members know that their contributions will be welcome and to underline the fact that differing opinions will be accepted. This demonstrates that the members of the group have an obligation to help to carry the program. Quality of participation is more important than quantity of participation. Participation can probably best be measured in terms of the kinds of contributions made by members of the group:

> Extent to which there is a flow from one idea to another.

Degree to which members of the group are applying the content to their own concerns and interests.

Manner in which they are furthering the thinking and understanding of the group.

To participate verbally it is first necessary to participate by listening to what is going on and to understand what is being discussed. Only by intelligent listening will a contribution further the discussion and work towards the goals of the group. Some members of the group participate most helpfully when the group is bogged down, others when things are going smoothly. Some can act best as authorities and resource people, others as persons who raise doubts and questions. The same person may not even participate in the same way on two different days. The basic information surprise pattern (teachable moments) of group life is that which encompasses a solution pursued to its successful conclusion.

The content and purpose provide a focus for the group effort. Every group is organized around or within some specific content and has a goal which involves that content for some purpose. If the group is really working toward an accepted goal, then information has some relevance to all of its deliberations. Information may make different demands on both the group and its initial leaders; but in general it is centered around the following considerations:

Need for good listening.

Need to read in order to have a common focus for discussion.

Value of general participation and the sharing of ideas about important matters.

No one is the authority. All are authorities as citizens. Resource persons may be invited in from the community temporarily.

All share the responsibility to inform themselves, to think critically and independently.

Discussion groups may eventually lead into action groups. Action results also as members participate in community life.

DISCUSSION PATTERNS

Eventually, as the participants realize the power of information to support some desirable action program, they may be willing to accept the discipline of an organized viewing, listening or reading program. When participants have been helped to an appreciation of their purposes and roles they may be ready to accept the following guidelines for discussion groups:

Read the assignments carefully. They help focus discussion on important issues.

Speak your mind freely. The discussion meeting is yours — a chance for you to say what you think. Say it, no one has your background and experience.

Listen critically and thoughtfully to others. Try hard to get the other person's point of view. See what experiences and thinking it rests on. Don't accept ideas which do not seem to have a sound basis. On almost every question there are several points of view.

Strike while the idea is hot. Don't wait to be called on before speaking. The idea you have will either be forgotten or will be presented by someone else if you wait.

You are discussing. This does not mean that you must reach decisions or agreement. Action results only as members participate in the community as citizens or as members of other groups, clubs, organizations, associations.

In the beginning, the discussion group focused upon cognitive issues may be similar to a formal class in its dependence on the leader and in the lack of knowledge about and suspicion of fellow members. Gradually as the members come to recognize each other as persons and enjoy being together, the leader becomes more of a resource person than an authority symbol. Eventually the group activities, and the statements of the authors being read, take the center of attention.

The leader, of course, needs considerable skill and confidence, and probably a more thorough subject knowledge than is needed in most other teaching methods. Learning takes place as individual needs are met and the process becomes active rather than passive absorption. Discussion

patterns help participants learn how to improve their content analysis
and communication skills. The emphasis in group training is on the
helping skills; setting up an agenda, helping group members work through
conflict, testing for group consensus at any given time, supporting new
members, assisting a group to clarify where it is in a problem-solving
sequence, and increasing other members' willingness to express frank
opinions.

Every group is studying something, be it only themselves, or the
process in which they are involved, or subject content in relation to some
problem, or community context. The content is always unique to the group
discussing it and to the things which the group want to keep in mind for
doing an effective job. The work of a study-discussion group, as dis-
tinguished from any number of other kinds of groups, is the production
of a climate in which the understanding of each individual about a particular
problem or subject can be increased.

The problems which arise when thinking is done in a group, instead
of by an individual, are similar to the problems of doing any kind of work
in a group. The problems which the group faces in order to help them
solve their work problems are shaped by the kind of work to be done as
well as by the kinds of questions posed in the content being discussed.
A staff group trying to put together a radio show may give a very different impression of their work from that of the agency's board at an annual
meeting. Each group's tasks are different and make different demands
on them in order to get the work done. Similarly, a discussion of an
agency's purpose in the community will be different, at least to the individuals participating in it, from a discussion of United States foreign
policy.

Not only does the way in which the group must work differ, but the
way in which it does not work will tend to differ also. One group, for
example, may be involved in a discussion of family and parent-child relationships. The problem of parent-child relations may be so close to
home that all members of the group can personalize the discussion.
Participants will talk in terms of opinions and attitudes more than in
terms of rigid facts or detailed information. They cannot help but become personally involved.

In this situation, the leadership component will work to build a strong
group feeling which will provide acceptance for emotional statements and
for personal feelings, which are bound to arise in such a discussion. The
leadership component will probably permit considerable freedom, checked

primarily by the group itself, so that participants can discuss what is
really of concern and of interest to them. The usefulness of the encounter
may depend on the understanding of relationships which operate.

Conflicting points of view, in order to be fully understood, must
be analyzed in terms of the principles to which they appeal. For example,
a person arguing that right and wrong are meaningless in isolation from
society is appealing to the principle of social convention. An individual
who maintains that right and wrong are valid concepts independent of
time, place, and persons is appealing to absolute moral standards.

People who express the same views, as well as those whose views
conflict, may be appealing to different principles. In order to demonstrate
the relation between the points of view people express and the principles
to which they are appealing, it is essential to keep pushing back from
opinions or conclusions to principles:

What were the principles involved in the different points of
view on the question?

Did different principles always lead to different conclusions?

Is there any value in pushing back to principles when people
express the same conclusion?

What conflicting principles were evident in the group? How
were these differences handled by the leader and group?

Make sure that the discussion does not remain on the level
of opinion but keep pushing back to principles.

On the other hand, a group may be discussing problems of an agency
in the community. The problem may be a serious one but few participants
will necessarily personalize it. It will probably become apparent that
there is a need for more facts and information. Opposing positions
and points of view may be held by vested interest factions. Actual problems and other occurences may have to be identified and studied before
useful and intelligent opinions as well as points of view can be arrived
at or defined. In any event, this type of group activity resembles the
project work of an agency's professional staff.

CONTENT AND QUESTION ANALYSIS

The interest of the group may center upon a wide variety of content: novels or other works of the imagination, essays or opinion oriented material, factually oriented sciences, and the exposition of conceptual material. In any event, librarians are adept at least humanistically in the content analysis of materials. The content of the work will need to be analyzed for its potential value in promoting discussion. The following questions may serve in preparing for the communicative context:

Content Analysis

What are the important issues in the material? Are the issues discussable? Does the issue lend itself to reflective thinking?

What stems from the author's argument? Are the author's assumptions made explicit? Is the evidence adequate? What viewpoints are neglected?

Content Organization

What is the nature and extent of the problem? What let to the present situation?

How serious is the problem? What are the effects of it? Can the cause of the problem be removed?

What aspects of the problem present the greatest difficulty to the group and the community?

Content Presentation

Obtain information on all sides and aspects of the topic.

Into what main divisions can the topic be subdivided? Prepare a brief introduction to the topic.

Prepare pro and con questions on the different phases of the problem or issue as a discussion guide.

However important content analysis may be initially, it is not of itself sufficient for communication. The content of the work will need to be analyzed for its potential value in promoting discussion. Preparation for discussion is not merely a list of questions. Do not hold

too rigidly to a prepared outline. Be ready to develop the discussion
in whatever major area of the problem the group might want to consider.
It is important to consider those aspects of the topic which are within
the knowledges, interests and abilities of the participants.

By his selection of questions for discussion and the sequence in
which these questions are asked, the leader can predetermine the kind
of discussion which will follow. He can, by choice of question, determine whether the discussion will deal with an examination of facts, with
an interchange about values, or with a free-wheeling analysis of opinions
held by the group. By the sequence of questions, he can also decide
whether discussion will move from facts to values and then to opinions
which grow out of these values; or whether, in reverse, discussion will
start at the point of opinions and then push back to values and facts underlying those opinions.

Although it is true that by his selection and phrasing of questions
the leader can do much to determine the direction of the discussion,
he must also reckon with the desires of the group. He may well decide
that he wants to move discussion from opinions back to values and facts
but the group might decide that they first want to discuss facts. If they
have been meeting together for some time they may well take the ball
away from the leader.

This suggests that the leader should discuss with the group his plan
of action and his strategy of discussion. In many cases it will be wise
for the leader to point out that he plans to move from facts to opinions
or vice versa. If the group disagrees and wishes to reverse the procedure suggested by the leader, it will probably be better to move with
the group rather than having the leader and group work at cross-purposes.

PROBLEM ANALYSIS

The central problem in communication is an understanding of what
participants mean when they are talking. No one participant can think
with another person unless he understands the other person's meaning.
Despite the difficulty, discussion very often has to proceed from assumptions which cannot immediately be investigated. In order to encourage and promote the development of leadership among participants
in the group, the initial leader must involve the group in the process of
continuous evaluation. The following points may serve as issues around
which discussion can be developed:

Was the group leader's introduction brief, impartial, and interesting?

Was the group leader's opening question designed to locate the interest of the group in the topic for discussion?

Did the leader follow-up and develop the interest of the group in the topic for discussion?

Was participation well distributed?

Were various sides of the question brought out?

Were the leader's questions stated impartially?

Did the discussion stay on the subject?

Was anyone permitted to dominate the discussion?

Did the encounter extend the present interest of the group in the topic or problem for discussion?

Was the group talking and working together in exploring the problem?

Depth of encounter: was there adequate development of the topic in relation to the amount of time available?

The leader can help in clarifying apparent or real conflict in the group by making certain that the words people use have the same general meaning for everyone in the group. He should continue to question a group member to find out what he really means, or to ask him to explain it in more concrete terms. Although this may be a fairly direct approach, the difficulty lies not so much in knowing what to do but in when to do it.

Probably the greatest difficulty in communication is language and its usage. A common ambiguity is evident when two or three people, one after the other, say essentially the same thing in a way that indicates that they are not aware of what has already been said. In trying to help the group with its own process, the leader may restate what one person has said or point out the similarity in a number of statements and suggest what is common to them. He has to be careful not to put ideas into other

people's heads. When the group's difficulty seems to involve a problem
of communication, it may be that participants:

Do not pay attention to what has been said.

Use the same words to mean different things.

Apply the same abstract term to different realities.

May be rambling descriptively or in a disjointed manner.

Verbal discourse may be at variance to nonverbally perceived
values.

If sufficient care is taken during a discussion to seek clarification
of abstractions, communication among the group may be considerably
enhanced. The danger of abstract terms such as "advocacy" is not that
they are abstract, but that they are often not explained by the events or
things in the real world to which they refer. The following example
may help to isolate and examine some of the difficulties which commonly
arise from discussing abstractions.

What do you mean by advocacy?
Advocacy means the preservations of human rights.

What do you mean by rights?
Those privileges we all have — man's inherent privileges.

Such as?
Liberty, for example.

What do you mean by liberty?
Religious and political freedom.

And what does that mean?
Political freedom is demonstrated when librarians work as
    advocates of the people.

A conflict may be on the superficial level of opinion or attitude.
It may be on the level of evidence, or the meaning of facts which support
the differing opinions. It may be on the deeper level of values or preferences. One difficulty to watch occurs when a group operates at the
same time on different levels and is unaware of doing so. One person
may be arguing that democracy is a wonderful thing, another person that
democracy will not work.

The phrasing of questions and the sequence of questions will determine the kind and level of interaction. Questions must be planned in
accord with the strategy for discussion. Probes should be made to determine the principles and values underlying statements. Apparent areas
of agreement (and disagreement) should be analyzed to determine the
extent to which real agreement or disagreement actually does exist.
The problem of strategy is half solved when this difficulty has been
given enough attention.

There can be nothing quite so confusing as to talk about a number
of overlapping issues as though they were the same. Once the group
agrees on the issue it is discussing, the problem becomes one of exploring differing opinions. Conflict generally starts at the level of
opinion when participants state widely different points of view. The
most common problem is that of starting with conclusions. If the reasons which support each opinion are not stated with the opinion, they
must be asked for. If each person is forced to state his position fully
(and given a chance to do so) the group can then assess how reasonable
the positions are.

Two generally encountered blind alleys are arguing about facts and
arguing about values. It is not very useful to argue about facts. One
can discuss the significance of a fact, or whether it makes any difference,
or its possible meaning. But if the fact itself is in question, one can
only agree on a way of finding out whether it is correct or not, or agree
that its correctness cannot be determined.

Values are a different problem. Personal preferences range from
minor tastes to beliefs in certain concepts, from a minor irritation
to the determination to destroy anyone who believes in a different kind
of social order. There is very little to be gained by arguing about preferences. Peoples' values can change in a group situation, but only
when the group can agree on a standard to which it can apply pressure
to conform.

In selecting questions, the participant can move in two directions:
either from facts and values to opinions; or from opinions back to the
values and facts on which the opinions are based. If he starts at opinions, however, there is very little that is truly educative if he doesn't
help to move the group back to a consideration of underlying facts and
values unless he is merely conducting a public opinion poll. In many
cases it is wise for the leader to point out that he plans to move from
facts to opinions or vice versa, and to sound out the group on their agreement to the procedure:

Decide what strategy of discussion to use. Should it concern
itself primarily with opinions, with values or with facts?
Should it move from one level to another, and in what direction?

Having decided on the basic strategy, select tentative questions
for possible use as well as the sequence of the questions.

Examine each question to make sure that it really does deal
with only one level and that the participants know what kind
of discussion is called for.

Make sure that widely differing points of view (if related to
opinions or values) are called for; and that, by the phrasing
of the question, judgments are not already made as to what
values and opinions are acceptable.

Do not suggest the answer in questions designed to get at
facts, but do state very clearly in what area or areas answers
are desired.

Participants in the group need to understand the manner in which
individual differences and varying backgrounds of group members bring
about differing interpretations and conclusions from identical facts
and data. Most often faulty reasoning occurs in moving from facts to
conclusions and from principles to opinions. Opinions or ideas offered
in a discussion should not be convicted, or acquitted either, without a
careful look at the evidence on which they are based:

Facts offered either justify the conclusion or are insufficient
and irrelevant.

Use of an authority as evidence is justified by the qualifications
of the authority. Is his statement supported by evidence or
based only on opinion?

Examples offered as evidence are valid in terms of their re-
presentativeness (one sample of anything is almost meaningless), and their relation to the issue under discussion.

Most conclusions and opinions are based on underlying premises
which are often imperfectly stated and can easily lead to confusion.
Giving of an opinion without reasons to support it neglects to provide
a basis for forming a judgment. Ready and unanimous agreement on

a controversial issue indicates nothing more than that it is easy to agree on conclusions for significantly different reasons.

Logic is not concerned with the truth of statements; it is only concerned with whether they relate consistently to one another. Logic always says, IF such-and-such is true, THEN something or other follows. It works the other way around. Instead of starting with a general proposition, one can start with particular cases and generalize from them in an attempt to establish a law. This process, called induction, is subject to many errors although it has proved a valuable way of proceeding for both the physical and social sciences.

When a familiar image or experience is employed to explain another more difficult idea, the assumption is made that the two things are alike enough to enable one to transfer meaning from one to the other. It would be simpler to conduct an argument without using analogy; and one can make a case for denying the use of analogy in discussion. Although analogies can mislead, they can also be a powerful stimulant to imaginative thought. The following cautions may be considered:

Whether the two circumstances compared are really similar.

Analogy may disregard fundamental differences and stress only superficial points of similarity.

A general rule cannot be based on an analogy from a single example.

Does one event cause another? Many things vary in the same direction and at the same time, but there need be no causal relationship between them. Someone in the group needs to be tough about this element of the discussion by raising a question about any blandly stated causal connection as to whether:

Asserted causal connections can be really demonstrated.

The cause is sufficient to produce the effect, e.g., the export of potatoes from Idaho can actually have very little to do with the frequency of bombing in Cambodia.

Other factors may operate which might be a more important cause than the asserted one.

To help group deliberation, the leader at various times may have
to make sure that people distinguish between fact and opinion in the arguments advanced. The following cautions may be observed in the content analysis of any message whether in dynamic or static composition:

> Opinions are neither accepted nor dismissed without careful
> consideration of the reliability of the evidence, and the logic
> or illogic of the reasoning.

> People should state all the premises from which they are
> arguing.

> Analogies are used and weighed with caution.

> Cause and effect relationships stated or implied are examined
> critically.

> The group continues to push back to causes.

> Each point of agreement and disagreement is noted and
> clarified as the discussion moves along.

Information exists nowhere except in the minds of people. As a
result, the knowledge being discussed in a group session is in a kinetic
not a logical state. The cognitive, affective and, possibly, skills domain
of any one participant are in dynamic disequilibrium at any point in time.
Resolution if at all possible is but a momentary plateau which may be
sought for and achieved only by the use of dynamic methods of clear
reasoning and critical thinking. But the results may well be astonishing
because communicative activity of this kind can predispose a broad range
of human beings to accept and exploit for their pressing concerns and interests the logical and deductive infrastructure which media, library,
and information resource specialists have created.

SIX

RETRIEVAL MODELS AND STRATEGIES

It is difficult if not impossible for a group qua group to retrieve information, although the participants acting in concert may develop the prescriptions for a search protocol. Even in a highly disciplined research team, individuals are usually assigned tasks to search, retrieve and bring relevant information back to the group. With the groups and individuals which the resource specialist usually negotiates, information supply has to be considered as a learning imperative. Demonstration may be undertaken and indeed repeated over and over again with the participants.

Unfortunately, many resource specialists are not as sophisticated as they could be in the complexities of search and retrieval, let alone consider the process as a mode of problem solving and thinking. The look-up skills are fairly commonly practiced but when it comes to the negotiations of index space they do not understand the complexities involved, nor the opportunities offered by the hermeneutic (explanatory) power of the system, even though that system is a product of their own making.

Index space, as distinct from message space, is the totality of methods and devices by means of which the patron is led from the individuality of his concerns and interests to some location in the materials collection where he can peruse relevant data. Index space includes any means by which the patron is led to some data that has surprise value to him. The explanatory power of the hermeneutic system (index space) is not always evident; and the patron may require some tutorial instruction on how to use it effectively (109):

The boundary between index space and message space is difficult to locate precisely in practice. On the one hand, the unsophisticated patron may have to go all the way from a card catalog in a library to the shelves and delve through the pages of several books before anything will arouse his interest. On the other hand, the more sophisticated patron may be quite surprise at the coordination of two or more terms juxtaposed with the regressive feature of the descriptive entries which he finds at the subject file. In this instance, he may have "retrieved" all the "data" he requires and need not consult any documents at all.

Considerable confusion and some "mystery" has been allowed to creep into the reference retrieval process and its relationship to advisory counseling. While there may be some minor differences in emphasis, the function of one is but an extension of the function of the other. Whatever difference there may be lies less in the role of the professional communicator than in the purpose of the patron. An ordinal display of the types of requests may look something like the following:

Simplest, most direct and most frequent request is for an individual book. The reader knows the author and title more or less precisely. Shelf classification is simply a locational device.

A specialized book by an author is requested. The catalog again is an aid, but more emphasis is placed on classification to bring like books together.

The elementary subject approach to books is a request for any good book on a certain subject. The alphabetical subject catalog primarily serves this purpose.

The next step is to select the best book on a certain subject which meets the readers purpose. A reading list may be provided which treats different aspects of the subject.

An extension of the previous request is the person who requires material selected from related special classes. This utilizes the classification which assists the reader and the reference librarian.

The request is purposeful, definite and extensive. A search requires comprehensive subject bibliography and the catalog. All available resources whether in the library or in others, or those in related subject fields, are examined.

Search for knowledge that does not now explicitly exist, but which is made evident in the coordination of classes and in the operations on propositions. The result is an insight — a solution which can lead to an hypothesis. Based upon a conjunction of classes, a relationship becomes evident from perusing the document abstracts. The hypothesis is then verified through the usual research designs.

Patrons are encouraged to seek help by an accepting attitude and relaxed atmosphere which permits the communicator to give undivided attention to the patron. A questioning look addressed to a patron browsing in the reader interest collection may induce a request for help. The patron may be wandering around the facility, paging through a book here or turning catalog cards there with apparent frustration. Eventually, he will usually turn to the professional communicator who is nearby and indicate some interest.

At this point the patron has entered the system and he may want to move in any of a variety of directions. By means of the informal nondirective interview, the patron is able to identify and discuss his concern or interest. It appears to the communicator that this patron has thought about the constraints and opportunities embedded in his problem situation. The reasonableness of this hypothesis is further strengthened by the fact that the patron has been browsing in that category of the reader interest collection related to his concern or interest.

The communicator may wish to strengthen the probability that the hypothesis is accurate by steering the intervievee for a few moments towards the display or exhibit associated with an appropriate category of the reader's interest browsing area. The exhibit, to be effective in this area, will have to be focused on a display of materials as elements representative of the reference form divisions of the browsing topic. Even though the display may be changed frequently, the elements are always suggestive for follow-up by the patron. According to Shores (130), Table 4, Inquiry and Reference Form, identifies the resource structure underlying any subject approach to message space.

Any exhibit associated with a topic in the reader's interest browsing file may be displayed in this fashion and indeed, in fact, is programmed to help the patron move from an identified and specified concern or interest into the reference retrieval (RR) collection. The RR collection is a traditional attempt to organize a part of the materials collection in a manner that is more relevant to the behavioral transactions of the patron's environment. The RR collection is representative of the totality of human knowledge but organized in a way that is typical of human inquiry. The categories are identified in Table 4.

Table 4
Inquiry and Reference Form

INQUIRY TYPES	FORM MATERIALS
Definition, spelling, abbreviation, symbols, foreign terms usage	Dictionary
"Something about," general information, self-education	Encyclopedia
Current events, past year's developments, recent happenings	Yearbook, serial
Notables, specialists, socialites, others	Biographical dictionary
Locations, descriptions, distances	Gazetteer, atlas
Addresses, purposes	Directory
Curiosities, statistics, events, formulas, allusions	Handbook
"How to do," "How to make"	Manual
Reviews, best books, subject literature	National, trade, subject, bibliography
Pictures, cartoons, slides, films, recordings	Audio-visual material

REFERENCE RETRIEVAL

In those instances when the patron is ready for it, the communicator's interview moves from a nondirective to a semidirective mode. His hypothesis has been strengthened as the patron begins to respond to questions which may lead into probable areas of reference retrieval concern. In other words, the patron becomes aware of inadequacies in his cognitive ("information") map and this awareness stimulates him to consult reference sources. The interview components or questions of the communicator "spontaneously" grow out of the typical form divisions of human inquiry:

Language is one of the most persuasive facts of existence and is used in every contact between individuals. Questions about meaning, spelling, pronounciation, usage and synonymous words are common. Abbreviations, signs, and symbols occur frequently in contemporary fast-paced societies. Mobility and plurality of interests in society produce interests in slang, dialect, foreign, and other new words.

Bibliographic location inquiries seek readings, viewings and listenings about topics of interest which may be used at home over extended periods of time. The readings sought may be current or retrospective and the location of the source document is important after the identification and selection have been made. One or several books, films, recordings may be sought. On the other hand source location questions may include such parts of bibliographic units, as poems, plays, essays, articles, stories, editorials.

People inquiries cluster around types of interest and involvement in society. Notables may be living or dead and include statesmen, soldiers, explorers, scientists, athletes, artists, philosophers, religious leaders. Specialists may be occupied in the sciences, humanities, social sciences; or in the professions of law, teaching, engineering; or in the trades, business and industry. What are the facts about these people, their dates of birth and death, degrees earned, names of wife and children, present address?

Place, location and description questions and the determination of distances between them have increased markedly as a result of the immediacy of mass communication and the growth of world-wide aviation transportation. Curiosity has been widely

stimulated about cities, islands, mountains, streams, lakes,
and other natural or man-made points. More recent astron-
autical voyages have stimulated interest about the expanding
universe.

Organization of man's efforts has rapidly increased. There is
a constant need for agency names, addresses, rosters of officers
and members, purposes, publications, qualifications for membership. There are a variety of agencies. Learned societies
are devoted to research and development. Professional, political and trade associations are concerned with the promotion
of services. The institutions of education, welfare and culture
include colleges, universities, libraries, museums, observ-
atories. Firms may be commercial or industrial. Clubs continue to proliferate for both men and women.

Current events may be so contemporaneous that a report of
them has not yet appeared in book form. Inquiries abound
for information about events being reported in the daily news.
Less frequently information will be sought from records
published contemporary with the past event. The inquirer
may be doing original research, or the report of the event may
never have found its way into book form, e.g., find an eye-wit-
ness account of the first world's heavyweight championship
fight?

Background and trend questions have two elements in common:
background information first and separate facts incidentally.
Summary source may be espeically prepared for the layman.
The element of recency is the most common characteristic of
the trend question. These inquiries involve current developments in specific areas of human activity which are more recent
than the background inquiry.

Facts and activities constitute a preponderence of questions and
include curiosities, statistics, literary allusions, law and order
and documentary inquiries. Activity questions include the "how-
to-do," "how-to-make," "how-to-perform." Questions of this
type revolve around domestic matters: food and cooking, home
maintenance, first aid. Particularly significant is the desire
for illustrative matter about the activity, whether audio or
visual.

The citation retrieval strategy differs from the inquiry abstract and reference retrieval (43). Instead of a group of terms which leads to an interface with a part of knowledge, citation reference begins with a group of author's names who are making important contributions to a subject specialization. With this group of names it is possible to trace significant developments in the field. The subject specialist can be expected to know the important names in his field, even though it is not possible to do so beyond his own subject area.

Historically, the scholar, in the Renaissance sense, knew all of the specialists at work during his epoch. Scholarship was the contemporaneous concern of a limited number of the intellectual elite. Once, however, the printing press had proliferated knowledge, specializations gradually developed until, by the end of the nineteenth century, universal knowledge was no longer within the grasp of any one individual and scholars knew by name only those working in their own field. Name citation entry to knowledge became limited in scope. For all other areas of knowledge it was imperative to use subject aspect entry.

Term entry, commonly called subject headings, originally developed from proletarian roots in community library service. The common man serviced by the emergent public library movement could not be expected to know the names of any scholars. Indeed he quite likely knew the name of no author whatsoever. But the common man had concerns and needs for information expressable only in topical format. Subject headings grew in response to requests for specific information closely related to the work life of a people. As the educational level of the nation grew and the interest patterns changed, subject heading work grew more complicated until it is now the concern of systems analysis.

Reference retrieval resembles a problem-solving situation. The identification of objectives, the statement of goals and the working out of a plan are essential characteristics of negotiation. Negotiating a solution to an information problem depends largely on the resource specialist's ability to induce the patron to agree upon a search action that will result in information acceptable to him. Search action is based on information about the patron's total problem and the rules of the library and information science game.

The search strategy is the outcome of a position analysis or group of tentative decisions on where the librarian and patron stand and on how specific developments will be handled when they occur. The resulting tactics are the means for reaching a solution for each sub-problem. Rigidity of approach must be rejected and the search strategy has to be

placed on a situational negotiation of resources. Variations will always
occur which make the shape of one situation different in degree from all
others.

More extensive information negotiations may justify a written analysis.
The position analysis serves as a continuous reminder of the objectives
and goals to be accomplished and is especially valuable when doing a
literature search for a group of specialists. It serves as a frame of
reference or point of agreement to which the group may return when new
areas of disagreement or confusion in resource potential arise.

The interface process between the patron and the professional communicator is flexible and dynamic. In other words, it is cybernetic, involving the patron at any point of contact and at any point in time. In
effect, the interpersonal interface explicates a series of feedback loops
either implicitly or explicitly built into organized message and index
space. Through involvement with a wide range of developmental and
encounter materials, the patron is assisted to achieve maturity in self-
control and self-design. The following outcomes may serve as an illustrative summary of skills required to open up the environment of information, library, and media centers for the individual patron:

If unfamiliar with original sources, refer to secondary ones:
compendia, indexes, bibliographies, and mediagraphies for
guidance to primary sources.

Begin with most recent sources and work back to ensure accuracy of developments and statistical data.

Use document index, checking all topics from specific to general as well as related terms through the cross-referencing
system.

Table of contents may provide an outline of the subject to compare and contrast with the "relative" indexing approach.

Consult the introductory pages for terminology, methodology
and another viewpoint; footnotes for scope notes and citation
refinement; back pages for addenda, errata and appendices.

Watch for trends and related, supplementary and contradictory
facts; for data which can be correlated, juxtaposed or projected;
as well as weigh each note against the needs and goals of the
search project.

Recheck the original search ptotocol and consult with other involved persons for policy and implications for supplementary
or possible substitute information.

Note and check each source for all necessary facts. Take
notes or abstracts systematically and in adequate detail.
Make sure that citation and paging are accurate.

These induced learnings may be considered to be the behavioral outcomes of instruction in library use (109). In addition, there are a wide
range of search and retrieval skills which are taught to patrons, sometimes by tutorials, but preferably, so the profession maintains, through
an instructional enterprise. The search and retrieval skills are based
upon the strategies required to scan the logical organization and indexing
of message space. There are, in general, two prototype strategies
based upon the way knowledge is presented and stored in the RR collection.

Reference retrieval includes two models whereby the patron assisted
by the communicator can interface with organized message and index
space. Because it is related to transactional behavior and activity, the
first model is the simplest and most direct. Data retrieval is a direct
entry into a lookup document file frequently arranged by outer form as,
for example, in a traditional reference collection. Shores (130) provided the initial conceptualization of typed questions upon and for which
the major focus of reference retrieval occupies the attention of information, library, and media specialists.

The reference retrieval collection is fairly simply organized and
can be readily related to the transactional behavior of daily life. The
remainder of organized message space within the media, library or
information center being larger in size and more complete in organization
is more difficult for the patron. This collection is arranged by subject
and topic which seem to be far removed from the concerns and interests
of daily life. Not only is the notation abstract, but the syndetics is difficult if not impossible for the patron to follow.

SUBJECT RETRIEVAL

The flowchart model has been developed as a second aid for the communicator in helping the patron employ the total collection in the center
for reference retrieval. The flowchart bears a relationship between the
patron's inquiry and subject space which is analogous to the displayed
form divisions that exhibit relationships between the reader interest

classification and the reference retrieval collection. In any event, the function of the flowchart method is almost identical with the first model which is reference retrieval. Of cource, variations and combinations can be made of the two models into any number of specific retrieval flow charts, a method originally developed by Carlson (24) and displayed in Figure 5. In either instance, data or materials are retrieved by means of a lookup strategy which combines subject content with reference form as indicated by Shores (130):

> For language questions involving meanings, spellings, pronounciations, word usage, abbreviations, signs and symbols, slang, dialect, names and foreign terms, consult dictionary sources first.

> For background questions, involving "general information" or "all about" inquiries, consult encyclopedias first.

> For trends questions, involving records of progress, last year's happenings, and current events, consult continuations and serials.

> For fact questions, involving curiosities, statistics, documents, allusions, dates, literary items, and activity questions involving "how to do" or "how to make", consult handbooks and manuals.

> For questions about persons, places, and agencies, involving biography, addresses, location, and distances, consult directories first.

> For questions relating to the location of materials such as books, essays, poems, plays, short stories, speeches, articles, and original reports of research, consult bibliographies and indexes first.

It was at this point in the majority of instances that traditional librarianship terminated the helping interface. Only in recent years, under provocation from information science, has the interface relationship attempted to promote critical and creative thinking on the part of patrons. Before proceeding to an identification of the final two models of search strategy, it might be well to pause at this point and attempt an interim summary integration of the benefits which the patron is expected to receive from the reference retrieval interface:

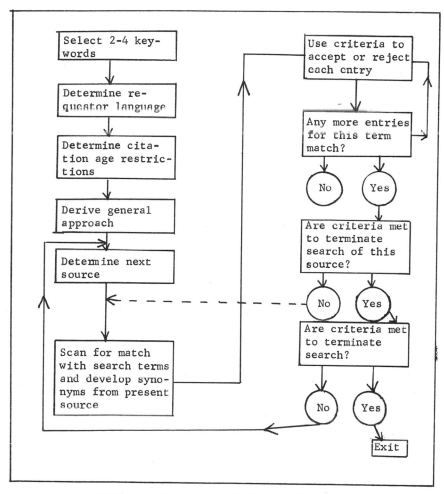

Figure 5 . Generalized Reference Retrieval

Identify the information needed that is pertinent to a given
problem. Decide on the related resource materials.

Learn to browse for a human interest topic and its form divisions in the reference retrieval file in order to choose documents which will contain needed data.

Learn to use the indexes and catalogs for lookup retrievals
and find appropriate resources whether on the premises or
out in the community.

Select appropriate topics to search for in the document index
and find pages on which information or surpriseful data can be
found.

Skim the material to see if it is adequate in order to bring new
information to bear on the problem context.

Read, view or listen in order to take adequate notes, organize
data and reach conclusions as well as make a bibliography
of sources and materials.

Eventually, perhaps as a result of experience and repetition
of the above search patterns, learn to browse in the index
file in order to correlate coordinate terms and the regressive
relationship between descriptor set and class mark on any
unit card.

In addition to the above taxonomy of behavioral outcomes, elaborate
instructional programs have been developed in certain parts of the profession. It is for the first two retrieval models that instruction in the
use of information, library, and media centers is almost exclusively
concerned. For some reason, not entirely clear in professional literature, instruction is truncated at this point and either or both the
specialist and the machine take over. It may be that the composition
of the mediation process whether by machine or specialist is considered
to be too complex to be taught to the general public. If so, the communicator has a responsibility to see that popularizations, whether in programs or in publications appear in the public domain.

Reference retrieval is employed as a method of thinking by which
the patron can begin to appreciate the distinction between the aspects
of a topic (subject) and the topic itself. In the majority of instances,

the patron is initially preoccupied with aspects of some topic not yet
clearly specified. He is immersed in the context of a life situation
whose emotional and transactional aspects overshadow to the point of
obliteration any clear apprehension of a subject in the abstract and
logical sense of a subject indexer. Using reference form based on inquiry types, the communicator has a powerful method which accepts
the patron approximately where his thought patterns are (inquiry form
and aspect) and moves him to a subject descriptor orientation where his
formatted inquiry has to be for information (data) retrieval.

In order to benefit from reference retrieval and exploit the surprise
values of the data obtained from information retrieval, it is assumed
that the patron has brought affective and cognitive concerns into congruence. This means, essentially, that he has described, analyzed and
identified an interest or concern. It assumes that the words used are
congruent with his feelings on the matter and that this congruence has
been worked out intrapersonally in his own mind or in a catalytic interface with an interactive communicator. This assumption has, of course,
been made explicit in the foregoing chapters, but given the actual inservice practice of traditional specialists, the importance of this behavioral development cannot be too strongly emphasized.

SEARCH AND DISCOVERY

Reference retrieval is a mode of patron assistance that represents
a necessary but transitional phase of development between the initial
counseling or audiovisual therapy interview and the eventual process of
information (data) retrieval. It is difficult, if not impossible, for the
majority of patrons to make the leap without a method which combines
some behavioral aspects of life situations with the more abstract and
conceptual manipulations of information retrieval. Reference retrieval
works from reference form materials based on inquiry types to the coordination of subject descriptors for logical retrieval strategies and
back again to the methods of a subject indexer when describing, abstracting
and typing a document.

The third model of search and discovery as a retrieval strategy is
a significant departure from the previous models. It is employed when
searching document pools whose contents are classified under terminology control. The traditional classified catalog and the modern subject
thesaurus are logical and deductive systems. Each term whether in
symbol or verbal notation is precisely defined and its relationship to
other terms is neatly identified. The relationship between two or more

variables is displayed based upon knowledge as created by the disciplines and as subject analyzed in document pools.

These distinctions and relationships among variables both dependent and independent can be retrieved by coordinating the control terms in logical strategies as developed by Kent (79). Consequently, the research specialist for whom such strategies have been primarily developed has a powerful tool at his disposal. However, insight into intuitively new relationships among variables comes "ex post facto" as a result of reflection upon the product of the search rather than as a result of dynamic involvement in the process.

It may be debatable whether the fourth model is a distinctly different search and retrieval strategy from the previous one. It may even contain the genesis of an instructional design for teaching the use of the third model as a cybernetic retrieval strategy. As conceived by Fairthorne (36) it had elements of both perspectives. But as applied by his followers, it unfortunately became involved with the assignment of roles and links to materials rather than, as it were, to the minds of users. In order to realize its power as a cybernetic retrieval strategy, the patron may require training in the literature of classificatory assignments as developed by Merrill (93), Metcalfe (94), Sharp (126) and others because there is as yet no "popular" introduction.

In any event, this cybernetic retrieval strategy is a more sophisticated search tool and requires that more instrumentation be supplied by the infrastructure technicians in information, library, and media science. Additional specifications include some indication of author's viewpoint (perhaps modified roles and links) which makes it possible for the patron to engage in an exciting and stimulating involvement with knowledge made dynamic. Traditional instrumentation has provided a document class mark and this is reflected in document pools with relative shelf location. However, where classification has been emancipated and documents are accessioned it is difficult to learn to engage in discovery retrieval unless an abstract is included on the unit card record.

Discovery retrieval is based on the fact that it is possible to assign (classify) an author statement (document) to almost any subject in knowledge as determined by the author's point of view. For example, an author's treatment of "water" or practically any other topic can be assigned to any one of the Dewey classes. The author's viewpoint is the determining criterion and an appropriate class mark may be designated for that descriptor in the subject abstract. The unit card records are

organized in the subject file under a particular descriptor. In scanning
this file, the patron can compare and contrast varying class assignments
for the n-set of document cards filed under the regressive feature of one
descriptor. Other descriptors on the unit card records range widely.
As those are noted, many questions arise in the mind of the patron which
may develop into valuable insights among the variables.

The search and retrieval skills including both document and subject
file analysis are of fundamental importance to the effective utilization
of an information, library, and media center by any patron.   The profession maintains that while some skills may be acquired in the discovery
contexts of materials activity and production, effective growth in skill
ability is largely a product of instruction and evaluation. The nature of
an organized materials collection which is subject analyzed, indexed,
and classified constitutes an environmental constraint. Of course, the
individual may master any constraint on his own, given the necessary
motivation and perseverance. However, the complexity of an organized
collection in any information, library, and media center is such that
training in its use can facilitate matters.

There may be relatively few patrons whose critical and creative
thinking require the use of higher order search and discovery models.
Usually decision making will take place on a much lower level of integration and the reference form question stance of the communicator's
interface will suffice. But the communicator cannot ignore higher order
levels of integration and should at least be prepared to move patrons to
greater maturity if motivation can be made to occur. By means of cog-
nitively oriented and probing questions, the interface can be expanded and
extended to higher levels of thinking such as interpretation, application,
analysis, synthesis and evaluation.

The ordinary librarian is not prepared to give this kind of service.
There are few if any librarians who ever browse in the subject index,
let alone know how to ask questions which will extract surpriseful data
from index abstracts and unit catalog cards. In fact, the librarian has
no theoretical position nor even principles which would guide him in
understanding the epistemological value of the products of his subject
indexing and classification. Usually he is much too involved with the
reading and memorization of the contents of books to be bothered with
such abstract matters.

The communicator has an appreciation of index space and an understanding of the abstract representations or unit subject cards which on
a mere lookup basis lead to the surrogate experiences and knowledge of

document message space. But browsing in the index space of unit subject cards alone can lead to insight for analysis and synthesis nowhere
as readily obtainable from the classified document store. Careful perusal
of the entries under descriptor can take into account the varying syndetic
features of each descriptor set in relation to the regressive functions
of class mark and document title.

Evident form divisions help to lower the level of abstraction in the
descriptor term and assist in understanding the application of the topic
to whatever contexts can be identified in title statements. Point of view
is evident in class work which can be compared and contrasted with other
titles and class marks. The descriptor sets as recorded on each unit
card can be employed to reveal the consistency and logic of the knowledge subsystem being exposed. A comparison of the structure of this
subsystem with the variant points of view may reveal the relation of
fact and hypothesis, trends in data, cause-effect relationships.

Obviously, browsing in index space is hard work. It is natural to
want to reach for a book that will actually do the work for the patron.
But no abstracts or guides are written for topics as they may be for subjects. As a result, the librarian has ignored this type of helping service
for the patron. A great deal of the power of the indexing and classified
model provided in the subject catalog remains unused and thus wasted
for all but an infinitesimal number of "sports" or users who are extremely
atypical.

The subject content of knowledge upon which reference retrieval
operates is the totality of knowledge or message space. The patron's
inquiry as it is identified, analyzed and abstracted from the life situation
within which it is embedded, is brought into the focus of awareness as
a topic which can be related to subject knowledge. Using the behavioral
cycle as a guide, the communicator encourages the patron to describe and
analyze the context of his concern until it can be succinctly stated as an
inquiry which can be negotiated in the subject file.

Content may be anything, including oral language, and nonverbal
and audiovisual message space which upon observation appears to have
a pattern and which can be analyzed for retrieval purposes. The usual
content upon which reference retrievals are done is the organized discourse unit of human language. Subject content is the evidence of human
perceptions which have been modulated by language in oral or written
format and developed into the observations and judgements of sustained
discourse units. The content analysis employed is both inferential, to

identify author's intentions, and descriptive or reductive (precis writing) in order to abstract a descriptor set from the document.

CONTENT ANALYSIS

Content analysis is certainly not foreign to library science, indeed analyses of content in some form or another constitute an integral element in the librarian's daily professional work. Content analysis is a central concern of both the library and information processing professions. Without content and its analyses there would be no selection, no subject indexing, little information retrieval and transfer or reader services. Content itself is the message space of the library's collection. The collection and its message contents constitute an essential link in the chain of events which relates communicator to receiver. Attention to this particular link in the communications cycle consumes a considerable portion of the communicator's professional time.

By revealing the probably intent of the message sender or the possible effect upon receiver, content analysis can provide a more accurate and reliable description of communication messages. Content analysis research exists almost in symbiotic relationship with audience research. A basic relationship is presumed to exist between a communications' message and the characteristics of receivers who abstract and index it in their minds. Analogous to this phenomenon, professional content analysis looms as a large and ever-growing enterprise in the information transfer endeavors of contemporary society. In the words of Allen Kent (77), professional content analysis would be trivial, "(a) if each event impinging on the consciousness of any human being would result in identical streams of observations; (b) if each observer would use identical words in identical configurations to describe each such single event; and (c) if each human being interested in learning of the event would phrase questions using identical terminology."

Professional content analysis is concerned with the transfer and use of information as requested by an individual who interrogates a store of documents. He wants to receive such information (selected from various senders) as will determine to his satisfaction some anticipated personal form of activity or cognitive state of affairs. The interrogating organism has a readiness to respond. The information obtained and judged to be relevant (i.e., its surprise value) determines the form of activity or state of affairs which occurs.

Information impact affects the interrogation-receiver in some choice
to be made or in some other way, and the extent to which the receiver
is affected depends upon the amount of information obtained from any one
message unit or any combination of message units. There is obviously
a difference of kind and/or degree between the inquiry initiating status
of an interrogating organism and the goal-state to which he aspires.
Information is sought, analyzed and used in relation to the degree to
which the interrogating organism moves from an initiating or interrogating
status towards a desired solution situation.

In his work the professional content analyst is constantly preparing
for communications situations in which a receiver initiates contact with
the source(s) and as such reverses a significant aspect of the usual
model of communications relationship between sender and receiver. In
the traditional models of communication, the sender transmits a message
through a channel, perhaps to one person as receiver but most often,
unless the message is stictly a private affair between intimates, trans-
mission occurs in a one-to-many relationship, and in a rigorously hier-
archical format.

Retrieval systems provide on demand and with maximum precision,
information related to the questions posed by individuals. Logical relationships ordinarily constitute the criteria of validity when tested in a rigorous manner. However, the question of relevance is another matter
because the efforts at behaviorizing message and index space have so
far been unsuccessful. The document drops which may be logically valid
will have to be examined in a communicative context which includes the
intrapersonal negotiation skill of "reading the document technically."
As the tactic cycles, data is displayed in variant aspects which cause information surprise in the mind of the receiver-negotiator.

In his receiver initiated communication there is a one-to-many mapping
in a direction opposite to that of the more familiar communications sender
system. The receiver interrogates many sources, some or all of whom
presumably could yield the sought-for surprise values. However, in
most instances, the interrogator does not use the entire message of any
one sender and he may not find his desired information in any one source
but only as a product of all the sources consulted. This model of communication has a considerably different pattern from that of the traditional
sender-receiver model. This model is concerned with question coding
when working with a patron and message coding when indexing documents
in preparation for service to patrons seeking information.

CONTEXT ANALYSIS

The context and source of a question is as important as the nature of the interrogation itself because it is the context from which the question arises which determines the relevance of document drops. Data will surprise only to the extent that its value can be perceived in relation to the opportunity set evident in the context.   There are, in general, two types of contexts which differ in kind: the happening and the planned event (Figure 6).   The impromptu happening occurs in the countless situations of daily human activity.   In addition, there are numerous occasions when a planned communications event will initiate questions in the receivers.

METHODS	COMMUNICATION TYPES	OBSTACLES
Planned event: create situations for involvement and feedback	S R R R R	Receiver may lack interest and motivation
Impromptu response: nonverbal and audiovisual contexts lead to verbal and organized message space	S S S S R	Inchoate need and incongruent goal

Figure 6 . Planned vs. Impromtu Event

Questions grow out of the way each individual has of perceiving nature and, as a result, the retrieved response to questions may not always be relevant. Questions result from fundamental hypotheses in the requestor's thinking and shift from one hypotheses to another as perceptions continue to occur. The initiation of communication, or interrogation as it is usually called, by a person approaching an information retrieval system is based upon verbalizations peculiar to his own thinking. The problem occurs because professional service is based on a retrieval communication system that can be triggered into operation by the verbalizations of requestors rather than by the authors of communication's messages stored in the system.

Information science uses content analysis for its potential ability to place some cybernetic control on knowledge growth and development, as

well as to expedite the transfer of information based on retrieval strategies
and indexing efficacy. Information science endeavors to organize the denotative aspects of language while its connotative aspects remain a formidable problem in any efforts to formalize natural language, and formalized it must be, at least to some extent, so that retrieval reliability
is at least somewhat predictable. Denotative reduction as in an indicative
abstract can be treated by logical methods but, of course, does not include the connotative reduction or informative abstract of the source's
intentions about his subject. The informative abstract summarizes not
the subject, but what the document says <u>about</u> its subject and, as such,
would appear to introduce inappropriate elements into indexing languages
and schemes for retrieval purposes.

In information science, indexing languages serves as the major method
for subject description and, to a more limited extent, subject control.
Indexing provides a common ground or code between indexer and searcher.
Indexing language makes it possible to format the content of both documents and search prescriptions and thus secure a maximum matching of
the two in retrieval operations. Indexing develops and fixes the specification of content by some descriptive labels and arbitrary notation. Content analysis is thus antecedent to the assignment of any descriptive labels
to the document and is related to the perennial problems of materials
selection and materials subject analysis. The end result of the selection
and analysis is to label the content of documents in such a way that informative statements may be generated in response to questions posed
at the file by patrons.

Operational use of content analysis does not attempt to substantiate
inferences about the intentions and concerns of the sender. While some
work has been done on the predictability of flagging terms (subject
headings, descriptors) for information location, this project work cannot
be considered as research and inferential verification. It specifically
serves as an infrastructure for information gathering and literature
synthesizing purposes. Such flagging devices may also serve in the
browsing process, or the preeducative and prescientific foraging operations so essential in laying out one's thoughts about "felt" needs and in
symbolizing the "need" so that it can be mapped onto the retrieval system.

Subject analysis, subject classification, retrieval and guidance are
almost exclusively concerned with labeling meaning for retrieval and
consequently suffer from all the limitations, elusiveness and weaknesses
of that approach. Content analysis is expressed in subject headings which
include hypotheses about use, or transactional meaning, as opposed to

descriptors (descriptive of content) and in document location classification which also includes reader interest, or transaction meaning, i. e., how documents are used, not only how content is described. Such is the unique feature of reference retrieval collections organized by the inner and outer form of the materials themselves (138).

The media, library, and information processing professions are concerned about such activities as materials production and selection, subject analysis of documents whether for indexing, subject heading or classification purposes, and retrieval strategies. It is not normally expected that any research inferences will be made on such analyses, even though many judgements over selection are made about documents such as author viewpoint, propaganda and treatment bias. However, judgements such as these are in the nature of appraising fidelity of communication, i. e., its clarity and value for communicating a particular message to the patron. Selection especially serves the purposes of identifying the nature and extent of filters in the message and clearly is also closely related to language composition and critical and creative exposition.

Despite the great deal of analysis of content which occurs every day in the media, library, and information center little attention has been given to the research use of it in order to achieve the purposes of a systematic and quantitative discipline. Such use would describe more accurately the status of subject literatures, the various media productions and materials, and audience publics as well as the changing boundaries among many subject fields. Cross media analysis is an area of pressing concern, particularly in determining which subjects and presentations are treated more adequately in various media materials. Comparisons could be made in terms of depth of analysis, of interpretation, scope of coverage and additional aspects which may unfold as surpriseful to various types of patrons. Of equal value and significance is the use of comparative analysis with a single medium.

So little is known of the comparative accuracy, completeness, authenticity and reliability of popularizations or digests as compared with the original that it is difficult to guide judgements about the appropriateness of such materials for various types of users. Content analysis can have a disciplinary effect upon the otherwise disparate efforts of the resource specialist by forcing him "inside" the content in a way that his usual reading and his usual impressionistic analyses do not. The simple frequency-count of quantitative content analysis may open up new aspects of a document which even the habitual book reader might otherwise miss. The comparative analysis of one book with another can reveal recurring patterns which a single reading would not uncover; and when the experience is cumulative it can provide better insight and give additional dimensions to the information specialist's own reading experiences.

Cross-media analysis can, of course, investigate such transformations of phenomena that are isomorphic and/or homomorphic. But this approach apparently relates to the ways in which the same thing may take on different appearances, as when a subject or one of its topics can be presented variously in formats such as bibliography, dictionary, handbook, encyclopedia. But there is a distinction between the outer form of appearances and the inner form of subject concentration where differences are brought together in the same conceptual scheme. Cross-media analysis is a matter of cross-organization where linkages are developed between message systems composed of different kinds of phenomena. This process is indicative of the symbolizing and systemizing process that is represented by the cybernetic behavioral cycle of the adaptive control organism.

SEVEN

INSTRUCTIONAL DESIGN AND DEVELOPMENT

Communication is the socially relevant endeavor of creating the
human conditions within which information surprise can occur, be pro-
cessed cybernetically, and applied with or without instrumentation in
problem solving formats to social concerns and interests. The professional catalytic agent operates on two levels of interpersonal encounter:
one to solve the immediate need for congruence in the patron's request
for information; and — the larger goal — to develop a total personality
as outlined in the communicative aims of a particular agency or the communications profession as a whole.

The objectives of instruction in the use of media, library, and information centers can be extrapolated from the general communication's
objective of the profession: promote the maturity of individuals, groups
and communities (104). Maturity is engendered when the patron is assisted
not only to retrieve data from message space but also to negotiate the
surprise value obtained from that data and participate in a continuing
plan for problem solving his way through life. Problem solving requires
an experimental approach, a cognitive flexibility and a motivational pattern to become widely informed on the part of the citizen.

The purpose of communication is to create an open environment where
all citizens regardless of race, creed, or education can express themselves
freely based upon a developing ability to negotiate message space. Instruction in the use of media, library, and information centers is one
method employed by communicators to free the individual patron from
a fear of the complexity of organized message space. Instruction and
tutorials develop and strengthen the individual's innate ability to enter
the document pool at any point and negotiate his own way to any other
point with a minimum of mediation by instrumentation and infrastructure
specialists unless he chooses otherwise. A recent statement has put
the matter in perspective (63):

Reader education programmes need to be seen as part of the
total teaching-learning process. This involves real integration
into teaching programmes. It requires the development of cooperative relationships with teaching staff - dialogue, co-operation

and involvement in the planning of their programmes, and of reader education programmes. There is a need to differentiate between reader education and library instruction. These are separate functions but both are considered to be relevant at the tertiary level. Library instruction is seen to be concerned with the mechanics of library use whereas reader education is a more sophisticated and continuing process. Clarification of aims and objectives is necessary in relation to this.

While these sentiments may constitute desirable objectives for "library" instruction and "reader" education programs, it is quite another matter to assemble a group with whom to accomplish such goals unless the instructor has a captive audience. All too often, discussion of library use instruction and "reader" education programs begins with the assumption that an audience is assembled and eager to receive the library message. This approach neglects the fact that people must be motivated to participate before they can ever be motivated to learn.

There is often a feeling of frustration and bewilderment when the resource specialist is faced with the imperative to develop an instructional program. Basically there are two modes of procedure through the preliminaries, which can be extensive, before the eventual program series can be scheduled. The instructional designer can start by assembling an audience or participants if it is small group activity, or else he can start with an idea such as an issue or a concern which may have arisen from his program of monitoring the community. In either instance, the program of motivating participation is the central issue which these two modes of procedure are designed to solve.

MOTIVATING PARTICIPATION

The communicator who would recruit an audience or participants for small group activities must be able and eager to "rap" on almost any subject under the sun. Like the pied piper, the power of his rhetoric and the persuasiveness of his interests must be based upon wide reading, viewing and listening. Like the civic club speaker, he must be able to say enough on any topic which comes up to entice the listener(s) towards continued interface and participation.

In order to assemble a group, the communicator must first recruit participants. Various means may be used to call attention to the library's group programs like television and radio announcements, and newspaper articles. Some effective ways of reaching lower income areas are to

contact unions, put posters in public places like supermarkets, put notices
on bulletin boards of housing projects or using city directories for direct
mail.

Personal contact is the best approach. Telephone a potential member and ask for a personal interview. No method has ever been found to
be more effective than a face-to-face contact. Personal conviction about
the proposed group activity should be evident in the tone of voice, facial
expression and choice of words. Any sales talk should be personally
adapted to the response of the prospect.

Recruiting can never ba a mass enterprise. It is highly specialized.
Much attention must be given to detail. Each person is an individual and
should be treated as someone having important differences from any other
person. Names of potential members simply as names are practically
worthless. Other pertinent facts must be discovered: special interests,
abilities, and skills; memberships in other organizations; activities in
the community; friends and business associates.

Recruiting should be as decentralized as possible. It is much easier
to work in a neighborhood, social circle or business firm. Names of
potential members should be assembled for contact on the basis of related
interests. Send the prospective member publications that will interest
him and tell him about the agency and its activities. Do not send him
too much — just enough to intrigue and make him want more. Invite
him to some social function.

There are usually many reasons which motivate people to desert their
roles as solitary information seekers and become parts of the group activity. Such reasons may include the need to belong, or to establish friendly
social relationships. People may seek an opportunity for status, personal
recognition, or self-expression. In the process of satisfying such motivations,
the individual may learn to discuss rationally and purposefully, an outcome
which can be used to contribute to effective participation in community
life and to personal growth.

There is a popular fascination with group activity which makes the
process an important force to consider in the communications programs
of the media, library and information profession. This fascination both
attracts and repels the individuals involved with group dynamics. The
communicator soon finds, however, that the initial urge on the part of
any participant soon gives way to some worry over how his individual
self comes through to other people. His mannerisms of behavior and

speech are considered from the supposed effect they have upon the others in the group. Elements of the hidden agenda include the following problems:

Identify: Who am I in the group? Where do I fit in? What kind of behavior is acceptable here?

Goals and Needs: What do I want from the group? Can the group goals be made consistent with my goals? What have I to offer to the group?

Power, Control, and Influence: Who will control what we do? How much power and influence do I have?

Intimacy: How close will we get to each other? How personal? How much can we trust each other? How can we achieve a greater level of trust?

Socialization may never be "complete" but at least when it has been accomplished, to the extent that individuals in the group can work together, it is possible for the group to consider undertaking further activity of a "productive" nature. Productive is used only to indicate that the group as a whole may begin to impinge on the external environment and work in unison in a way that is analogous to that of an individual alone.

Initially, as a group begins to form out of conversational encounter situations, the members cannot be expected to do any "homework" in the sense of reading, viewing and listening assignments or information retrieval strategies. The content of the group conversation will be based on the opinions and ideas of the members supplemented by the communicator. Increasingly, however, as the communicator employs "book bait" techniques, the members may be motivated to undertake some sustained reading.

Kind of participation may well change as the sessions develop. In the beginning, participation may be an important factor stimulated by the leader, primarily to ensure that group members know that their contributions are welcome and to underline the face that differing opinions will be accepted. This kind of participation is a demonstration that the members of the group have an obligation to help to carry the program. Also, it may be important to look for simple situations which will permit the more shy and retiring members of the group to talk so that they may have the satisfaction and security of knowing that they can participate.

Effective and intelligent listening as a means of participation cannot be over-emphasized. To participate verbally it is first necessary to participate by listening to what is going on and to understand what is being discussed. Only by intelligent listening will a contribution further the discussion and work towards the goals of the group. Different people contribute in different ways. Participation by all members cannot be uniform or standard. Some members of the group participate most helpfully when the group is bogged down, others when things are going smoothly. Some can act best as authorities and resource people, others as persons who raise doubts and questions.

Group meetings constitute one of the best techniques for coordinating the work of various participants in program planning. Merely going through the motions of coordination will not suffice. All members, and especially the "supervisor", must ensure that human interface problems are resolved. Data confrontation will not solve human difficulties. Continuous feedback will indicate which tasks should be augemented, which decreased or modified, so that the program can run smoothly and efficiently. Indeed, each participant must promote the conditions which constitute effective group project work:

The current status of the program, its specifications, changes and information about the person(s) for whom it is being designed or made available to all members as rapidly as possible.

Frequent meetings are held to review progress or the lack of it in the program as a whole and the work of individuals. Interface problems are identified and quickly resolved. All participants work to make meetings productive:

Suppress discussion which has little bearing on the work of the project.

Analyze presentations in order to understand the essential situation and problem.

Investigate possible alternative solutions even if at first they appear to be insignificant.

Present at any appropriate time in a clear and impersonal manner the status and problems of their own work.

Identify the work of other project group members and
give credit for contributions made.

All members, but especially the program "supervisor", write
the specifications for each area of responsibility and each interface as soon as possible.

Each participant can receive without delay memoranda of any
program meeting. Included in these memoranda are brief
summaries and problems discussed, major events that have
occurred, and especially decisions and assignments made at
the meeting.

Starting with an audience may also encompass large segments of
the population such as labor, disadvantaged, aged. These publics can
be fairly clearly identified by demographic, socioeconomic, and cultural
characteristics. Once identified, these characteristics have to be trans-
formed into educational and information needs. The following steps in
the procedure constitute the basic method:

List the characteristics of that segment of the population
over which you are concerned.

Restate these characteristics as informational and educational
needs or interests.

Who besides your population segment also needs to know about
the needs and interests of your segment of the population.

What does each of these other segments need to know about
your segment of the population.

When, where and why will you assemble each of these segments
of the population.

When, where and why will you assemble your segment of the
population.

In starting with an idea or concept, the more controversial the concern the easier it will be to arouse interest and motivate many people to
participate. But it must be rememberd that controversy is largely an
extrinsic motivational device. As such, controversy alone will either
dissipate an audience or destroy the instructional vector. The power

of the controversial entry can be realized to better advantage in the programatic question: "who needs to know what" about the idea. The "whos"
and the "whats" can be identified and assembled in a variety of program
designs.

The formula "who need to know what?" is taken as the prototype of
the various questions asked in the process of interpretation. The question looks relatively simple but very soon the activities implied by it and
the interpreted data take on dimensions that were only latent in the initial,
and what soon appears to be a global formulation of the question. Volun-
teers and professionals are suddenly plunged into the whole area of communications and, in particular, into those two concerns which lie at the
heart of communication services to the public: audience research and
content analysis.

Community concerns and the interests of various publics usually
become evident when the question, "who needs to know what?" is asked
about each of the findings in a community study. "Who?" may be answered
in a number of ways: the general public, a defined group in the population,
people responsible for action, such as government, agency, or institutional
officers, organization leaders, key people. More than one such category
will usually be listed in response to the question of "who" as well as in
response to "what." The answers to "what" fall into several categories:
the factors and implications in the situation (information and understanding);
knowledge of accepted practice in dealing with it; adequacy of present resources; availability of state and national resources; experiences of other
communities in dealing with a similar concern.

In the past, librarians have been fairly circumspect in their response
to community issues. They have been largely content to provide materials
to meet demands and, where controversy has emerged, have struggled
to preserve their dignity and intellectual freedom. In a few instances,
there have been some attempts at program development which have been
known as adult education. However, in order to satisfy those citizens
of a more Machiavellian turn of mind as well as meet pragmatic questions
of vested interest, program negotiation cannot be ignored.

PROGRAM PLANNING

It is impossible to effectively move from the initial phase of motivating
to participate directly into the learning enterprise of instructional sequences
such as units and lesson plans. An intermediate phase cannot be ignored
which is called curriculum design in formal education and program planning

for the more informal adult involvement.   The former may be done by
one teacher or a small instructional team; whereas in the latter instance,
as many of the adult participants should be involved as possible.

As a basis for program planning, the coordinator and participants
should gather all possible facts through existing community agencies
or other types of local resources which relate to group wants, needs
and interests (105).   In order to be effective, program development has
to center on controversy and activism as the core of its planning.   Communicators have long ago taken the position that controversy and anxiety
pave the road to active participation and crucial learning for the vast
majority of people in any community.   Such an orientation may be anxiety-
producing for the average librarian, but there are a number of steps
which can be taken in planning effective programs:

> Analyze your own resources as a program coordinator as well
> as the resources and equipment of group members of the com-
> munity.
>
> Inform yourself and the group about the real conditions sur-
> rounding the general content of a proposed program.   If it
> deals, for example, with city government, visit the various
> departments, read and collect all available materials.
>
> Consult specialists and resource persons who are familiar
> with pertinent activities and materials in the program under
> consideration.   Find out how other groups have carried on a
> particular type of program by means of visits to such com-
> munity agencies and groups.
>
> Assemble all available materials such as books, documents,
> charts, maps, that may provide solutions to problems arising
> in the program, using group members to aid in this work as
> far as possible.   Make the activities and experiences in a pro-
> gram as concrete as possible using illustrative materials,
> pictures, diagrams, charts, scrapbooks, posters.
>
> Have your group elect small committees which can better
> aid in planning the detail of the work in a unit of the program
> series.   Any unit in the series should remain flexible enough
> to permit adaptations to meet interests and needs as they arise.

Program planning for various consumer publics is based on the concerns and interests which have been interpreted from the data identified and organized in a continuing community study. The community development enterprise grows out of the fact that much education is constantly going on in an informal way. Community development enhances and strengthens the behavioral learning which citizens gain from their own experiences, from each other and through discussion, problem solving activities, and observation. Resource specialists in media, library, and information science have finally begun to realize this approach identified by Lindeman (86) so long ago:

The approach to adult education will be via the route of situations not subjects. Our academic system has grown in reverse order; subjects and teachers constitute the starting point, students are secondary. In conventional education the student is required to adjust himself to an established curriculum; in adult education the curriculum is built around the student's needs and interests. Every adult person finds himself in specific situations with respect to his work, his recreation, his family life, his community — situations which call for adjustment. Adult education begins at this point. Subject matter is brought into the situation, is put to work when needed.

Additional structured learning experiences may be sought to the extent that these bear upon actual needs and interests which are awakened by some experience or by some individual. The organizing of communications experiences helps to overcome the shortcomings of trial and error learning. To the extent that a learning experience helps adults go from a need to a solution, it becomes satisfying. A citizen's educational "curriculum" includes all the activities, experiences, materials and exchange of ideas which are employed in a cooperatively planned program. The following principles may prove useful in developing programs for service publics:

Members of the group should participate in planning and developing work and communications activities by means of open discussion of any plans submitted by the resource specialists.

The total program series should be divided into units and subunits, so that the completion of each topic can provide a satisfactory feeling of achievement. The result is an increased interest in proceding to another unit and eventually

leads to the larger objective which was previously identified
for the program service to the user public.

In order that technical experience and specialized information
may be used in solving group problems, the leader and participants have a responsibility to supplement "common experience"
by that of experts and specialists.

While some leaders may tentatively do long-range planning for
the group, the immediate planning will shift with the progressive,
cooperative evolution of member needs and interests.

If the leader is an expert in identifying participant interests,
activities and experiences he may be able to win the confidence
of the group. In such rare instances, the leader may devise
and carry out an integrated course of formal nature which meets
the needs of the group.

Evaluation should be built into any program series and provision made for the continuous measurement of progress in
terms of goals determined or agreed upon by the group.

When organizing programs in the community, consideration
should be given to differentiation and flexibility in the offerings
made so that the needs of widely differing individuals, groups
and organizations may be served.

Instruction in library use is presumed to be a component in any program of continuing education for adults. It is a basic component underlying self-control and self-design in the patron. The patron requires
both counseling and tutorials, and to be involved in educational experiences that are integrated, demonstrable and graduated. Without such
involvement, organized message and index space remains a formidable
structure that has little if any relevance to the behavioral transactions
of living people.

The educational opportunity of media, library, and information
specialists may always remain in the realm of exhortation unless developed in a systematic way and based on the actual production of instructional materials. The resource specialist must have an understanding of
and professional commitment to educational theory, human development
psychology and instructional design before real change will occur. For
those who do indeed want to realize high objectives, the model has been
explicated by Cleary based on her own guidelines (27):

What does the learner need to know? (These are the agency's objectives, aims and purposes.)

Is there evidence in the material that the learner is central?

Is there evidence that the agency objectives center on society generally and the near community specifically?

Is there evidence that the objectives are expressed in terms of what others have done and thought?

What is to be taught? What basic philosophy provides the frame of reference for the curriculum?

Has there been consideration of such questions as: What is a good life? What is a good philosophy? What is a good school? What is the role of the school in developing a good person and a good citizen?

On what theories or viewpoints of learning has the curriculum been developed? What is the role of the teacher in the learning process?

Is there clear delineation of what is to be taught in terms of the learner's understanding, skills and abilities, and values? How are the learning experiences selected?

Have criteria for selection of learning experiences been observed, such as (a) relationahip to objectives, (b) level of difficulty, (c) variety and (d) class organization?

In presenting new learnings, is some attention given to such procedural steps as motivation, presentation, drill, evaluation?

Are methods and materials of teaching emphasized, such as discussion, field trips, use of resource persons, audio-visual, printed materials, lectures and group work? Is there information regarding the organization of what is to be taught?

Is there consideration of continuity, sequence, and integration?

Does the organization of what is to be taught emphasize concepts, values and skills?

Has attention been given in the organization of content to such ideas as proceeding from simple to complex, from near to far, from concrete to abstract?

Is the organizational structure built on lessons, topics, units, subjects, broad fields or undifferentiated structure?

What evaluation processes are emphasized? Are purposes of evaluation procedures clearly stated?

Do they involve efforts to determine to what extent children have learned? Check effectiveness of curriculum and teaching? Serve as a means of guidance, of public relations and of clarified purposes?

What kinds of evaluation procedures are used: situational questions, answers, behavior content?

Are attempts made to help children in self-evaluation?

What evidences are there that group processes have been used in developing the curriculum?

Is there any evidence of developing readiness or appraising attitudes toward curriculum change, of identifying tasks to be done, of continuing evaluation?

Broad generalizations have always been available about the need for instruction in information use so that the resource center can "truly become the core of the educational system." But such glib statements do not identify the specific purposes, methods and techniques of an instructional enterprise. They are either lacking or when available are applied in a haphazard manner. In his survey of the state of the art, Bonn (1960), identified the major problems facing the profession before adequate instructional systems could be developed (17):

To determine the abilities or skills which are actually needed by the users of resource centers at various levels of life development.

To specify what needs to be known about reference form, media-graphic control, subject indexes and classification.

To develop presentation devices and instructional messages designed on the basis of communication and learning theory.

To identify the training needs of the professional instructor and establish instructional programs for both preservice and inservice trainees.

Instruction in the use of media, library, and information centers is in the main an exegesis of an explanatory system that comprises organized message space and indexed information space. Through discovery involvement in nonverbal and audiovisual message space it provides for perceptual development, concept formation, and the decision processes which Cleary has succinctly identified in a set of skills (27):

Investigative and Research Skills: the ability to locate, select, organize, interpret, and summarize recorded information and knowledge; on the basis of accumulated evidence to clarify and build values and beliefs.

Problem-Solving Skills: the identification of problems; a statement of tentative solutions; the collection of pertinent data; the formulation of conclusions and generalizations on the basis of collected data; and the implementation of the possible implications reflected in the conclusions.

Planning Skills: the examination of alternative actions or decisions; the assessment of the possible results of alternative action; the determination of decision or action; the execution of the plan; and the evaluation of results.

Human Relations Skills: the continuous assessment of one's own attitudes, drives, motivations and values; the sharpening through practice of one's ability to judge correctly the motivations which activate others; acquaintance with the many possible reactions of others to a wide variety of situations; the testing of one's values on the basis of experimental evidence; and the judging of the variety of human perceptions to a given situation.

Discussion Skills: an open-minded search for fact and opinion; subjecting them to critical analysis with due consideration of one's values as well as those of others; clarifying opinion and belief as the evidence comes in.

Group Dynamics and Group Work Skills: an understanding and assessment of the interplay and relationships involved in group activities; a testing in action of a composite of skills in investigation, discussion, problem solving, role assumption, group planning and decision making, and the interpersonal relationships involved in the process.

Starting with an idea, or an audience, does not mean stopping there. One should not underestimate the need for showing as well as speaking. What is seen is as important as what is heard. Every visual must have a purpose, as indeed must every word, and be simplified to the barest essentials. It must be remembered that in the initial segment of every program, brevity almost to the point of labeling is essential for instant appeal. If the viewer is going to switch channels, he will do so in the first half-minute. To the extent that a program audience is articulate concerning its needs and interests, some individuals in the group should play an increasingly important role in determining the materials which will most adequately serve their needs and fulfill their interests.

Within limits of these principles, program materials should be determined cooperatively by both group members and leader. Participants should contribute according to their particular abilities, experience and special interests.

Where individual background, experience and ability in a group make classification desirable, materials of varying difficulty, or activities of differing types should be developed cooperatively with participants on the basis of interests, experiences or capacity to do the work.

Where materials and content are of a broad nature, program series should be built around emergency situations which can be identified in the life situations of participants.

Fitting technique to purpose is required because some plan and order is necessary in group activity in order to ensure purposeful communication. If meaning is allowed to occur haphazardly, it may at a later date have to be corrected. Efficiency in communication is accomplished by fitting appropriate technique to the specific purposes sought. Purposes can range over those which search for information, for understanding, for problem-solving, or skill development.

If information is sought in the communications situation, then one could consider as a technique a speaker who is informed and whose message is organized. As an alternative, one of the audiovisuals might be satisfactory — particularly a film, a videotape, or a slide presentation that can carry an integrated message. For a smaller group, the working paper can serve as a satisfactory substitute. When the panel used is of a symposium format, information can be communicated directly and be fairly effective.

If understanding is the purpose of the structured communication, then something more than the speaker, the film or the working paper is needed. These information techniques may be used as a brief introduction, but they should be supplemented by the panel discussion, role play and straight discussion. In these techniques, understanding is better achieved, because information is shared and considered from different points of view.

If problem-solving is the goal of the communications situation, then any of the techniques for information and understanding may be used to define the problem. Once defined and analyzed, it is commonly expected that some action will develop. In order to promote action, a solution must be worked out through the technique of a meeting structure. Consensus should be reached at each step of the agenda or else no final agreement is ever likely to occur.

If the development of a skill is the objective of the communication or the learning enterprise, then any technique considered above can be used as long as it leads to involvement. When a skill is developed, habit patterns are usually changed or new ones formed. Consequently, involvement in the skill-producing activity is of primary importance, and is induced most directly through techniques such as the case study, and extended practice periods.

MOTIVATING LEARNING

Only a neophyte might be pardoned for assuming that curriculum development or program planning is either a simple or a brief experience. The process is long and involved, and only a communicator versed in project work will ever complete the assignment with equilibrium and satisfaction.

Policies constitute the general method by which professional staff interface with consumer publics. Policy includes innovative professional

expertise subordinated to actual community needs and interests. Through
policy, the patron enters the system and by means of professional expertise is taken to any other point in the system he may wish to go. The
feasibility of policy has to be worked out within the present constraints
and resources and, as such, constitutes a significant matrix for continuing professional development.

In general, in order to promote communicative effectiveness, the
daily work of the specialist in media, library, and information centers
would improve with a major shift in emphasis from a subject orientation
to a problem orientation. Under problem orientation, the specialist becomes more aware of human needs which can be met through the application
of information and education. The professional can apply what he knows,
learn more and consult with others especially in project work. The longterm objective is to promote the maturity of the individual professional
as a creative and critical catalyst in the changing affairs of all citizens.

In other words, the patron's approach to the environment is transactional and behavioral (156). This negotiative perspective towards the
environment, including the infrastructure of message and index space
of necessity has to be related to the presentation system employed by
a communicator in some particular situation. Joyce (70) has identified
four models and a range of techniques which may be employed in each
model (Table 5). The four models can be explicated in terms of the
skills of a liberal education as "taught" by communicators in media,
library, and information science.

Social interaction, as a process, emphasizes the relationship of
an individual to society, and his immediate relationships with other
people. Social relations result from a process in which reality is socially
negotiated in order to improve interpersonal relationships. In this process the individual develops his own self and mind as well as learning
subject knowledge. For example, as a result of group encounter with
conflict situations, the participants are led to sources of knowledge which
may enrich personal values and reactions.

Usually some concept of the good society is posited as an ideal towards
which to move. Growth is engendered in democratic, problem solving
processes devolving around social issues. Revolutionary conceptions
of society may also serve as ideals in order to develop reform minded
and even revolutionary activists. This approach is often anti-institutional
and anti-definitional and tends towards the happening rather than structured learning environments.

Table 5

Instructional Models and Functions

Function \ Model	Social Interaction	Information Processing	Personal Development	Behavior Modification
Preview	Role identification and description	Goals and agenda outline	Counsel and guidance	Outline topic to be covered
Question	Suggests elements in situations	Identifies questions related to problem	Hypothesize steps to be taken	Pose questions in outline
Present	Role play and simulations	Problem analysis, brain storming and discussion	Demonstrate performances	Present topic by lecture, film, etc.
Summarize	Participants analyze and interpret behavior	Participants summarize and apply	Participant replicates or continues demonstration.	Recitation and analysis.
Test	Recall, relate and interpret previous behavior simulations	Pilot demonstration before general application	Compare and contrast with previous demonstrations	Text and review

Create and develop a social system as a democratic group
happening.

Describe and analyze the nature of social life and processes
in the simulation.

Engage in solving a social or interpersonal problem which
arises in the system.

This model frequently grows out of group dynamics and sensitivity
training sessions when the participants are ready to construct knowledges
out of reflection on their own experiences. In learning to work with groups,
the outcome almost by definition is not predictable. Success is seen
in terms of persuading participants to inquire into the nature of experience
and to develop personal would views. Exposure to resources and subject
knowledge may be wide ranging so that individuals will create their own
frames of reference and ways of ordering reality. The processes of
social action may be conceptualized in such a way that the emotional and
affective interaction may more readily be understood:

Interpersonal Development

Patron engages in a variety of communications situations and attains successive but individual levels of competence. At each level
or departure point, the librarian employing interviewing or discussion
skills helps the patron access his own level of development.

If the patron requires more support in this assessment at any level
than can be given by the agency professional, referral is made and contact established with a helping consultant, an accepting group, or responsive community movement.

Periodically, the patron is encouraged to join with other persons
in teams, seminars, or groups for the purpose of developing new
ideas or creating new programs. The most important criterion for
joining such groups is the prior attainment of suitable skills or knowledge relevant to the activity to be undertaken and the processes of
the group. Counseling for group processes is as essential as for
content.

As the patron develops into a resource person in his own right, the
professional communicator offers him the opportunity of conducting
sessions in the library's own programs of communications. Supportive counseling sessions as well as rehearsal demonstrations before
and after these leadership situations may be needed.

Periodically, the patron should have the opportunity of taking responsibility for the development and conducting of entire programs
whether on the media center premises, over closed circuit television
or through the channels of mass media owned by the network of media,
library, and information centers.

Eventually, when the patron had developed his ability as one of the
communications "elite" he may be able to take leadership in community development and movements.

Information Processing is a process by which people are taught
to handle stimuli from the environment, analyze problems, organize
data, generate concepts and solutions, and employ verbal and nonverbal
symbols in many common but individualized ways. In general, the process
includes the components of critical and creative thinking in the general
problem solving model. The goal is an integrated and functioning self
based on the patrons capacity to process and integrate information from
organized knowledge sources rather than an interpersonal environment.
Frequently, the knowledge disciplines are considered as systems for
processing information.

The problem solving model employed resembles the scientific
method of inquiry more than the decision oriented model of socioeconomic
conditions. The orientation leans to the conceptual and cognitive processes which may be simulated in computer patterns. Information theory
has emerged as an aid in the study of thinking and problem solving. As
the participant understands the processes and ideas of a subject discipline, he incorporates them into his own system and, as a result, be-
haves differently. There exist a wide range of applications, because
this model has had a considerable historical emphasis.

There are, of course, a number of versions of the general problem
solving model. The essential steps in the method were available in
antiquity and may be considered the applicative version of the logical
and deductive approach to inquiry. For the purposes of communicative
and instructional design in the media, library, and information resource
profession, the version as developed by Cleary (27) may prove most
useful.

The only exception to the prevalence of this situation is that of
Cleary who has made an outstanding proposal for a curriculum in the
skills of a liberal education as distinct from the content of a liberal
education which is so highly touted by educators everywhere. The

main topics or subjects of this curriculum in the skills of a liberal
education have been identified by Cleary (27):

Sources of information and knowledge.

Acquiring information and knowledge.

Locating resources in agency and community.

Selecting and using current materials.

Employing reference retrieval collections for the form type
of data.

Employing multiple source retrieval strategies.

Analyzing, evaluating and interpreting information.

Organizing and applying information in problem-solving
formats.

This statement of outcomes is a general list which Cleary has explicated. The enumeration is designed to be a comprehensive inventory
of the skills of a liberal education which every adult citizen should possess.
Other professions, such as school librarians, have provided developmental sequences of these skills learnings for the elementary and secondary school programs. But no one seems to have developed an instructional
program for adults, except possibly within the context of activism whether
evolutionary or revolutionary.

Personal development emphasizes the processes by which the individual constructs and organizes his reality around his own personality
and emotional life. The internal organization of the individual affects
his relationships with the environment and his own intrapersonal communication. Self-concept and self-image are explored in order to develop
a reality oriented viewpoint of self, social relations and information processing ability. Personal development is the source of educational (continuing) ideas, as, for example, in solving the developmental tasks.

In this process of individualization for the person or the group, little
if any advance planning can be done. Avenues and support may be provided,
but the patron largely determines the motivation, the values and the direction. Instead of teaching, one focuses on the nurturing potential of the

communicative or educational environment (conditions) which gently
nudge the patron. Interface techniques are adapted to the characteristics
of the individual in order to increase his personal flexibility and ability
to relate to others productively.

An environment (conditions) is created, matched to the way the
patron's personality normally relates to the environment so that he can
carry out his tasks in new and productive ways. The patron is in control
of learning activities and selects his own self-learning techniques. The
method is usually nondirective and facilitating in order to increase patron
capacity to reflect on himself and plan better conditions for his own self-
development. Changes in the self enable the individual to function in more
integrative and effective ways. Self-training increases the individual's
capacity to feel and receive experience from the environment, and develops warmer and more effective interpersonal relations.

Extrapolating from the objectives of the profession supported by information, library, and media science certain behavioral outcomes can
be posited. These are general accomplishments presumable common
for all citizens and would need to be individualized in specific instances.
However, a display of these ultimate objectives may present a system
which will yield specific instructional goals and learning outcomes desirable to a wide range of patrons. Based upon communication science,
the following components have been arranged in nominal and ordinal
array (104):

Intrapersonal Development

Patron appears before the professional mediator indicating some
interest. The professional catalyst conceives this contact to be
one of a series and inquires whether the results of patron's previous
contacts were satisfactory.

Patron is given an initial counseling interview in which information
about his interests, life goals and ability to use information sources
may be obtained.

In those instances where the patron is too inchoate to discuss deep-
felt concerns, audiovisual therapy or browsing in thematic displays
may need to be used before actually proceeding to the second step.

At this point, in order to understand the problem-solving model of
communication, the patron may need some instruction in the use of
library resources as a method of thinking.

Employing the general problem solving model, the mediating professional together with the patron proceeds to enlarge the encounter to include outer-form materials which are more contextually oriented than subject classified.

When the subject and point of view have been established to the patron's initial satisfaction, a retrieval strategy (based on a boolean or other logic) is developed to search the descriptor file.

Document drops are examined in a "technical reading" for their information surprise value. If the information is not satisfactory to the patron, the search terms are regenerated and a new search strategy developed.

When a match has been achieved between the patron's goals and the kinds of information available, the professional mediator suggests related concepts and contexts in the exit interview for possible follow-up activity.

Patron enters upon a program of continuing development either in cognitive content mapping or in an n-dimensional matrix of interlocking situations and relationships.

Employing the method of case-load, the mediating professional is ready on a continuing basis to assist the patron to enter the communications system at any point and be expedited to any other point he may wish to travel.

Since many sources are available they have to be carefully matched to the goal to be achieved and to the task conditions for which they are to be employed. For example, pictures and motion may be substituted for concepts. Dialog and group discussion may enhance the intrapersonal communication skills of reading, viewing and listening.

Behavior modification is categorized into specific activities and sequenced into small manipulative and reinforcing steps. The emphasis is upon the change of behavior which is frequently external and the obviously visible manners that can be learned in a program. In fact, programmed instruction has been applied to a wide range of fields of study. Both the stimulus and response is controlled so that feedback will reinforce behavior change. The emphasis is on visible behavior change by manipulating environmental variables.

The leverage of external control is given to the individual who by submitting himself to a deterministic formulation can increase his freedom through self-control. Instead of acquiring subject knowledge, the individual brings his behavior under environmental control. In other words, the subject is learned by doing or by practicing behavior modification and relationships with the environment. Environmental conditions are enhanced so that more efficient behavior modification occurs.

Instruction is conceived as the creation of conditions or environments composed of interdependent parts. Content, skills, instructional roles, social relationships, types of activities, physical facilities and their use constitute an environmental system whose components interact with each other to constrain participant behavior. Staton (134) has in-indicated the essential steps in the instructional methods which carry the participant through the psychological factors producing learning. This method keeps the presentation system focused on the knowledges, attitudes and skills to be acquired.

Preview the content of the session in order to orient participants to the presentation topic.

Pose questions which will guide the group in anticipating specific points to be covered.

Present the topic in a manner that is developmental in terms of participants' concerns and interests.

Summarize the topic covered in participant behavioral terms which will encourage response.

Test and evaluate the participant's retention and understanding of the material covered in the previous session.

The behavior modification approach to a presentation method resembles the traditional instructional enterprise. While the method has to some extent been displayed by the three (see Table 5, page 141) previously identified it does have the advantage of motivating participants to learn and to know that they are achieving progress. It is a systematic process with specific procedures for involving participants in the topic under consideration and exists in modified format in all communicative methods. Staton summarizes the method as follows (134):

The instructor begins the period with an explanation of what the period will cover; he raises questions in the trainees'

minds, giving them something to watch for; he explains each
element of people's psychological needs; he asks trainees to
interpret and apply these needs to actual situations they have
encountered on their jobs; finally, he leaves time at the end
to review the lesson of a week ago. In the process of covering
these five steps he insures thorough coverage of all six of the
psychological factors affecting learning, and keeps his instruction sharply pointed toward the over-all objective of skills,
knowledges, and attitudes which will result in better performance
of jobs.

EVALUATION AND PLANNING

There are no formulae to use in evaluation. No one person has an
answer which will serve equally well for all communicators and for all
communities or for all programs. There are, however, certain steps
which should be gone through before one can get an effective program
under way. To facilitate discussion, a series of questions can be employed which parallel the required steps in organizing a program:

What are the first steps you would take in setting up a program
for the group?

Do you know of any groups that are already organized who
might be interested? Who are they?

If you do not know of already organized groups, where would
you start to recruit members for a group?

In trying to set up a program, either through an already
existing group or through contacts with individuals, what would
you emphasize primarily in terms of stimulating interest in
the program?

What do you think about the various general methods which have
been suggested for recruiting participants, e.g., lay control,
the coffee house facility, the street librarian?

Where do you think you will plan to hold your program: private
home, library, or elsewhere? Why?

What aids will you want in getting your program organized and
under way (materials, consultant, brochures, lists)?

The communicator will want to develop in his own mind an understanding of the essential elements in small group activity. The elements identified will become policies for a systematic approach to his professional services and act as methods within which participants can interface with the communications process. Just as changing the elements in a chemical compound alters the substance, so the combination of group elements alters the ensuing dynamics. In any event, each of the following elements contributes its share to the movement and direction of the group and the group personality.

Programatic Aspects

Recruitment and promotional development.

Neighborhood dialog and radical audiovisual software.

Street information access and retrieval.

Inhouse service to patrons.

Articulation of behavioral transactions, concerns and interests.

Individual counseling and guidance.

Group conversations and sensitivity dynamics.

Introducing participants to resources and materials related to life situations.

Articulation of individual roles in the group process.

Fantasies about group dynamics.

Who should I pretend to be?

Whose appearance will I like or dislike?

To whom will I respond or should I talk to?

Will the leader like me?

Select content and subjects of concern by the activity of the group project work.

Retrieval profile for each participant.

Profile coordination for relevant materials.

Resource persons to whom referral can be made.

Goals and methods are determined by the activity of group project work.

Objectives whether to provide information, training or idea exchange.

Patterns of participant involvement in order to determine methods.

Sequence of sessions specified by the activity of group project work.

Three or more sessions in various formats.

Various functions of observing, data collection and analysis.

Sessions arranged in subunits for feeling of accomplishment.

Evaluation based on and largely confined to group identified goals.

Data collection and analysis.

Interpretation and evaluation.

Physical Aspects

Time: a group that meets in the morning looks different from one meeting at night. A night scheduled group is more informal, less structured and tense.

Length of time should be definite as well as an insistence on promptness.

Space should not be too big or too small for the size of group. Small group participants need to be near enough to touch and maintain conversational voice modulation.

Physical arrangements range from cushions on the floor to lecture hall format. If discussion is intimate participants will want to pull chairs or cushions together. If not, then a table may be required to reduce fear arousal.

Lighting should be provided by headlevel lamps not the institutional ceiling overheads.

Content and processes may be generated internally or externally and be structured or unstructured.

Members added to or absent from the group change the cultural and social history of the group to the point where it may become completely different from the original complement of participants.

BIBLIOGRAPHY

1. American Library Association, Libraries and Adult Education, Chicago, Illinois: American Library Association, 1924.

2. American Library Association, Present Status and Future Prospects of Reference Information Service, Chicago, Illinois: American Library Association, 1967.

3. Thomas E. Anastasi, Face to Face Communication, Cambridge, Massachusetts: Management Center, 1967.

4. William H. Allen, "Media Stimulus and Types of Learning," Audiovisual Instruction, 12:27-31, January 1967.

5. Edmund Amidon. Interaction Analysis. Reading, Mass.: Addison Wesley, 1967.

6. Lester Asheim, "Research in Mass Communication and Adult Reading," Library Trends, 6:120-40, October 1957.

7. Dean C. Barnlund, Interpersonal Communication: Survey and Studies. New York: Houghton Mifflin, 1968.

8. C. E. Beck, Philosophical Foundations of Guidance. Englewood Cliffs, New Jersey: Prentice-Hall, 1963.

9. Marc Belth, "Diogenes Ascending," in Patrick R. Penland, Advisory Counseling for Librarians. Bookstore, University of Pittsburgh, 1969,

10. Marc Belth, Education as a Discipline. Boston: Allyn and Bacon, 1965.

11. Alfred Benjamin, The Helping Interview. New York: Houghton Mifflin, 1969.

12. Elsa Berner, Integrating Library Instruction with Classroom Teaching. Chicago: American Library Association, 1958.

13. Norman Beswick, "Librarians and Tutor Librarians," Library College Journal, 2:12-23, Spring 1969.

14. Walter Van Dyke Bingham and Victor Bruce Moore, How to Interview. New York: Harper, 1959.

15. Ray L. Birdwhistle, Kinesics and Context: Essays on Body Motion Communication. Philadelphia: University of Pennsylvania Press, 1970.

16. Donald H. Blocher, Developmental Counseling. New York: Ronald Press, 1966.

17. George S. Bonn, Training Laymen in the Use of the Library. New Brunswick, New Jersey: Rutgers University Press, 1960.

18. Mabel Booton, "A Close View of Advisory Service in a Large Library," in John Chancellor, Helping Adults to Learn: the Library in Action. Chicago: American Library Association, 1939.

19. Harvie Branscomb, Teaching with Books. Chicago: American Library Association, 1940.

20. A. Buchheimer, "Development of Ideas About Empathy," Journal of Counseling Psychology, 10:61-67, 1963.

21. Mary Lee Bundy and Paul Wasserman, "Professionalism Reconsidered," College and Research Libraries. 29:5-26, January 1968.

22. Ric Calabrese, "Interaction Skills and the Librarian," Illinois Libraries. 55:8-11, January 1973.

23. D. Ewen Cameron, Psychotherapy in Action. New York: Grune and Stratton, 1968.

24. G. Carlson, Search Strategy by Reference Librarians. Sherman Oaks, California: Hughes Dynamics, 1964.

25. Elaine Caruso, Experiment to Determine the Effectiveness of an Interactive Tutorial Program. Ph. D. Thesis University of Pittsburgh, 1969.

26. Patricia Cianciolo, "Interaction Between Personality of the Reader and Literature," School Libraries, Spring 1968.

27. Florence D. Cleary, Blueprints for Better Learning. Metuchen, New Jersey: Scarecrow Press, 1968.

28. Charles A Dailey, Assessment of Lives. San Francisco: Jossey-Bass, 1971.

29. Edgar Dale, Audiovisual Methods in Teaching. 3rd ed., New York: Holt, Rinehart and Winston, 1969.

30. James Dickoff, "Theory in a Practice Discipline," Nursing Research, 17:415-435, 545-554, September-October, November-December, 1968.

31. Maryann Duggan, Final Report: Library Internetwork Study Demonstration and Pilot Model. Dallas, Texas: Southern Methodist University, 1971.

32. Hugh D. Duncan, Communication and the Social Order, New York: Bedminster Press, 1962.

33. La Vaughn S. Ericson and Jean Carmody, "Integrating Library Skills with Instruction," Wisconsin Library Bulletin. 67:23-26, January-February 1971.

34. Eric H. Erikson, Childhood and Society. New York: Norton, 1963.

35. Eric H. Erikson, Identity, Youth and Crisis. New York: Norton, 1963.

36. Robert A. Fairthorne, Towards Information Retrieval. London: Butterworth, 1961.

37. Lucile Fargo, Activity Book Number Two. Chicago: American Library Association, 1945.

38. Ann F. Fenlason, Essentials in Interviewing. New York: Harper, 1962.

39. John H. Flavell, Developmental Psychology of Jean Piaget. New York: Van Nostrand, 1963.

40. Jennie M. Flexner and Sigrid A. Edge, Readers Advisory Service. New York: American Association for Adult Education, 1934.

41. Carolyn Forsman, Crisis Information Centers: a Resource Guide. Minneapolis, Minnesota: The Exchange, 1973.

42. Robert Gagne, Conditions of Learning. 2nd ed., New York: Holt, Rinehart and Winston, 1970.

43. Eugene Garfield, "Citation Analysis as a Tool in Journal Evaluation," Science. 178:471-479, November 3, 1972.

44. Charles R. Gengler, "Developing Skills for Problem Solving," School Libraries. 15:31-35, May 1966.

45. Harriett Genung, "Can Machines Teach the Use of the Library," College and Research Libraries. 28:25-30, January 1967.

46. George Gerbner, ed., Analysis of Communication. New York: Wiley, 1969.

47. William Gray and Bernice Rogers, Maturity in Reading. Chicago: University of Chicago Press, 1956.

48. Samual S. Green, "Personal Relations Between Librarians and Readers," Library Journal. 1:74-81, 1867.

49. Lloyd W. Griffin and Jack A. Clarke, "Orientation and Instruction of Graduate Students in the Use of the University Library: a Survey," College & Research Libraries. 33:467-472, November 1972.

50. Belver Griffith, ed., "Improving Library Service to Users: Some Research Approaches," Drexel Library Quarterly. 7:3-69, January 1971.

51. Helen Haines, Living with Books. 2nd ed., New York: Columbia University Press, 1950.

52. Edward T. Hall, The Silent Language. Garden City, New York: Doubleday, 1959.

53. Jill Hamberg, Where Its At. Boston: New England Free Press, 1967.

54. Katherine Harris, "Reference Service in Public Libraries," Library Trends. 12:373-389, January 1964.

55. Robert J. Havighurst, Human Development and Education. New York: Longmans Green, 1953.

56. E. Heath, "Some Aspects of Reading Guidance," Minnesota Library. 22:33-34, Summer 1967.

57. Frances Henne, "Learning to Learn in School Libraries," School Libraries. 15:15-23, May 1966.

58. Caroline E. Hieber, Analysis of Questions and Answers in Libraries. Bethlehem, Pennsylvania: Lehigh University, 1966.

59. Felix E. Hirsch, ed., "Standards for Libraries," Library Trends. 21:159-355, October 1967.

60. Frederick Holler, "Library Material Without Instruction: A Disaster," Journal of Education for Librarianship. 8:38-48, Summer 1967.

61. Ronald A. Hoppe, ed., Early Experiences and the Process of Socialization. New York: Academic Press, 1970.

62. Cyril O. Houle, The Inquiring Mind. Madison, Wisconsin: University of Wisconsin Press, 1961.

63. Patricia Hudspeth, "Report on Reader Education Seminar," Australian Academic and Research Libraries. 4:25-28, March 1973.

64. Margaret Hutchins, Introduction to Reference Work. Chicago: American Library Association, 1942.

65. Gerald Johoda, "Analyzing the Reference Process," RQ. 12:148-156, Winter 1972.

66. Elaine Z. Jennerich, Microcounseling for Librarians. Ph.D. Thesis, University of Pittsburgh, 1974.

67. Alvin Johnson, The Public Library. New York: American Association of Adult Education, 1938.

68. Eloise Jordan, "Adult Reference Service and Reading Guidance,"
Illinois Libraries. 48:523-526, September 1966.

69. E. J. Josey, "Role of the College Library Staff in Instruction
in the Use of the Library," College and Research Libraries. 23:492-
498, November 1962.

70. Bruce R. Joyce and Marsha Weil, Models of Teaching. Englewood Cliffs, New Jersey: Prentice-Hall, 1972.

71. Alfred Kahn, Neighborhood Information Centers. New York:
Columbia University Press, 1966.

72. Robert L. Kahn, Dynamics of Interviewing. New York:
Wiley, 1957.

73. Robert L. Karen, Introduction to Behavior Theory and Its Applications. New York: Harper, 1971.

74. William A. Katz, Introduction to Reference Work. 2nd vol.,
New York: McGraw-Hill, 1969.

75. William L. Kell and William J. Mueller, Impact and Change:
Study of Counseling Relationships. New York: Appleton, Century,
Crofts, 1966.

76. James R. Kennedy, "Integrated Library Instruction," Library
Journal. 95:1450-1453, April 15, 1970.

77. Allen Kent, "Human-Information System Interface," in Lee
Thayer, ed., Communication Theory and Research. Springfield,
Illinois: Thomas, 1967.

78. Allen Kent, Information Analysis and Retrieval. New York:
Wiley, 1971.

79. Allen Kent, Textbook on Mechanized Information Retrieval,
2nd ed. New York: Interscience Publications, 1966.

80. William J. Kiefer, "Library Instruction," Catholic Library
Association, Proceedings, pages 60-66, August 1959.

81. Thomas Kirk, "Comparison of Two Methods of Library
Instruction for Students in Introductory Biology," College and Research
Libraries. 32:465-474, November 1971.

82. Patricia B. Knapp, Monteith College Library Experiment. Metuchen, New Jersey: Scarecrow Press, 1966.

83. Malcolm S. Knowles, Modern Practice of Adult Education. New York: Association Press, 1970.

84. Bartholomew Landheer, Social Function of Libraries. Metuchen, New Jersey: Scarecrow Press, 1957.

85. Robert Lee, Continuing Education for Adults Through the American Public Library. Chicago: American Library Association, 1966.

86. Edward C. Lindeman, Social Education. New York: New Republic, 1933.

87. Ellen McCardle, Nonverbal Communication. New York: Marcel Dekker, 1974.

88. Donald M. MacKay, Information, Mechanisms and Meaning. Cambridge, Massachusetts: MIT Press, 1969.

89. Lucy Maddox, Trends and Issues in American Librarianship as Reflected in the Papers and Proceedings of the American Library Association, 1876-1885. Ph. D. Thesis, University of Michigan, 1958.

90. Abraham H. Maslow, Motivation and Personality. New York: Harper, 1954.

91. David K. Maxfield, "Counselor Librarianship," Occasional Paper No. 38. Urbana: University of Illinois Graduate Library School, 1954.

92. Joost A. Meerloo, Conversation and Communication. New York: International Universities Press, 1952.

93. William S. Merrill, Code for Classifiers. 2nd ed., Chicago: American Library Association, 1938.

94. John Metcalfe, Subject Classifying and Indexing of Libraries and Literature. Metuchen, New Jersey: Scarecrow Press, 1959.

95. C. A. Michelman, "Counselor and Librarian," Library Journal. 78:291-294, February 15, 1953.

96. Charles C. Milford, "Amplifying Reference Work," PNLA Quarterly. 28:238-241, July 1964.

97. George A. Miller, Psychology of Communication. New York: Basic Books, 1967.

98. Margaret E. Monroe, Library Adult Education. Metuchen, New Jersey: Scarecrow, 1963.

99. Margaret E. Monroe, Reading Guidance and Bibliotherapy in Public, Hospital and Institutional Libraries. Madison, Wisconsin: Library School, University of Wisconsin, 1971.

100. Ellis Mount, "Communication Barriers and the Reference Question," Special Libraries. 57:575-578, October 1966.

101. New Jersey Public Library Association, Adult Education Committee, Readers' Advisory Service: A Librarian's Guide, n.p.; n.d.

102. William J. Paisley, "Information Needs and Uses," in Carlos A. Caudra, ed., Annual Review of Information Science and Technology. Vol. 3., Chicago: Encyclopedia Britannica, 1968.

103. Patrick R. Penland, Advisory Counseling for Librarians. Bookstore, University of Pittsburgh, 1969.

104. Patrick R. Penland, Communication Science and Technology. New York: Marcel Dekker, 1974.

105. Patrick R. Penland and James G. Williams, Community Psychology and Coordination. New York: Marcel Dekker, 1974.

106. Patrick R. Penland, "Counselor Librarianship," Encyclopedia of Library and Information Science. New York: Marcel Dekker, 1968-

107. Patrick R. Penland, "Educational Media and Technology," Encyclopedia of Library and Information Science. New York: Marcel Dekker, 1968-

108. Patrick R. Penland and Sara Fine, Group Dynamics and Individual Development. New York: Marcel Dekker, 1974.

109. Patrick R. Penland, "Instruction in Library Use," Encyclopedia of Library and Information Science. New York: Marcel Dekker, 1968-

110. Patrick R. Penland, Interviewing for Counselor and Reference Librarians. Bookstore, University of Pittsburgh, 1970.

111. F. B. Perkins, "On Professorships of Books and Reading"; William Mathews, "Professorships of Books and Reading," U. S. Department of the Interior, Bureau of Education. Public Libraries in the United States of America, Their History, Condition and Arrangement. Washington, D. C.: Government Printing Office, 1876.

112. William F. Poole, "Some Popular Objections to Public Libraries," Library Journal. 1:45-51, November 30, 1876.

113. John W. Powell, Education for Maturity. New York: Heritage House, 1949.

114. Sidney L. Pressey and Raymond G. Kuhlen, Psychological Development Through the Life Span. New York: Harper, 1957.

115. Reading Guidance Institute, Papers. Madison, Wisconsin: Library School, University of Wisconsin, 1965.

116. Theodore Reik, Listening with a Third Ear. New York: Garden City Books, 1948.

117. Stephen A. Richardson, Interviewing: Its Forms and Functions. New York: Basic Books, 1965.

118. Carl R. Rogers, Client Centered Therapy. New York: Houghton-Mifflin, 1951.

119. Carl R. Rogers, On Becoming A Person; a Therapist's View of Psychotherapy. Boston: Houghton Mifflin, 1961.

120. Samuel Rothstein, Development of Reference Services Through Academic Traditions, Public Library Practice and Special Librarianship. Chicago: American Library Association, 1955.

121. Samuel Rothstein, "Reference Service: the New Dimension in Librarianship," <u>College and Research Libraries</u>. <u>22</u>:11-18, January 1961.

122. Paul Saettler, <u>History of Instructional Technology</u>. New York: McGraw Hill, 1968.

123. Lois Sayles, "Teaching Library Skills Through Subject Matter," <u>Education</u>. <u>86</u>:412-416, March 1966.

124. Anita R. Schiller, "Reference Service: Instruction or Information," <u>Library Quarterly</u>. <u>35</u>:52-60, January 1965.

125. Wilbur Schramm, "Why Adults Read," <u>Adult Reading, Yearbook of the National Society for the Study of Education</u>. Chicago: University of Chicago Press, 1956.

126. John R. Sharp, <u>Some Fundamentals of Information Retrieval</u>. New York: London House and Maxwell, 1965.

127. Jesse H. Shera, "Foundations of a Theory of Reference Service" in <u>Reference Research and Regionalism</u>. Austin, Texas: Texas Library Association, 1966.

128. Jesse H. Shera, <u>Foundations of Education for Librarianship</u>. New York: Wiley, 1972.

129. E. J. Shoben, "The Counseling Experience as Personal Development," <u>Personnel and Guidance Journal</u>. <u>44</u>:224-230, 1964.

130. Louis Shores, <u>Basic Reference Sources</u>. Chicago: American Library Association, 1952.

131. Louis Shores, ed. <u>The Library College.</u> Philadelphia: Drexel Press, 1966.

132. Eleanor T. Smith, "Reader Guidance: Are We Sitting Down on the Job?" <u>Illinois Libraries</u>. <u>48</u>:527-532, September 1966.

133. Helen H. Smith, <u>Reader's Guidance Service in a Small Public Library.</u> (Small Library Project Pamphlet No. 8). Chicago: American Library Association, 1962.

134. Thomas F. Staton, How to Instruct Successfully: Modern Teaching Methods in Adult Education. New York: McGraw-Hill, 1960.

135. Elizabeth W. Stone, "Quest for Expertise: a Librarian's Responsibility," College and Research Libraries. 32:432-441, November 1971.

136. Shelly C. Stone and Bruce Shertzer, Fundamentals of Counseling. Boston: Houghton-Mifflin, 1968.

137. F. S. Stych, "Teaching Reference Work: the Flow Chart Method," RQ. 5:14-17, Summer 1966.

138. Elvin E. Strowd, "Readers' Services: One and All," Southeastern Librarian. 22:184-92, Winter 1972.

139. Mary J. Swope, "Why Don't They Ask Questions?" RQ. 12:161-166, Winter 1972.

140. Robert Taylor, "Information Search Strategies," in Patrick R. Penland, Advisory Counseling for Librarians. Bookstore, University of Pittsburgh, 1969.

141. Robert Taylor, The Extended and Experimenting College Library. Washington, D.C.: U.S. Office of Education, 1969.

142. Robert Taylor, Question Negotiation and Information Seeking in Libraries. Bethlehem, Pennsylvania: Lehigh University, 1967.

143. Ruth M. Tews, ed., "Bibliotherapy," Library Trends. 11: 97-228, October 1962.

144. Dorothy A. Turick, "Neighborhood Information Center," RQ. 12:341-346, Summer 1973.

145. Robert M. W. Travers, Man's Information System. Scranton, Pennsylvania: Chandler, 1970.

146. Bernard F. Vavrek, Communications and the Reference Interface. Ph.D. Thesis, University of Pittsburgh, 1971.

147. Sarah L. Wallace, Patrons Are People: How to be a Model Librarian. Rev. ed. Chicago: American Library Association, 1956.

148. Douglas Waples, What Reading Does to People. Chicago: University of Chicago Press, 1940.

149. Ruth Warncke, "Total Community Library Service," Utah Libraries. 16:12-18, Spring 1973.

150. Charles Warren, "The Place of Libraries in a System of Education," Library Journal. 6:90-93, April 1881.

151. Henry Weitz, Behavior Change Through Guidance. New York: Wiley, 1964.

152. Marvin E. Wiggins, "Development of Library Use Instructional Programs," College and Research Libraries. 33:472-479, November 1972.

153. James G. Williams, Investigation of a Model for a Generalized Information Retrieval Program. Ph.D. Thesis. University of Pittsburgh, 1972.

154. James G. Williams, Simulation and Games. New York: Marcel Dekker, 1974.

155. Louis R. Wilson, Geography of Reading. Chicago: University of Chicago Press, 1938.

156. Asahel D. Woodruff, "Behavioral Objectives and Humanism in Education," Educational Technology. 12:51-55, January 1972.

157. Asahel D. Woodruff, Teaching Behavior Code. Baltimore, Maryland: Multistate Teacher Education Project, 1968.

INDEX

Counseling interface, 21-27

Creative thinking, 115-119

Critical thinking, 115-119

Curriculum design, 139-148

Cybernetic cycle, 48-58, 115-119

Cybernetic encounter system, 71-78

Dale, Edgar, 41

Developmental Counseling, 21-27, 37-58

Developmental tasks, 2-5

Dewey, John, 40

Dickoff, James, 40

Discourse analysis, 34-36, 95-102

Discussion patterns (group), 92-94

Dyad relationship, 16-31

Echo question, 34

Edge, Sigrid A., 2(40)

Encounter system, 71-78, 139-148

Environment, Transactional, 7-8

Environmental surveillance, 8-9

Expectation question, 33-34

Extension question, 34

Evaluation, 54-88, 148-151

Fairthorne, Robert A., 116

Fargo, Lucile, 73

Feedback cycle, 31-34, 110-111, 115-119

Fenlason, Ann F., 17(38)

Fine, Sara F., 83(108), 87(108)

Flexner, Jennie M., 1, 40, 73

Flowchart, Retrieval, 111-115

Form divisions (Classification), 107-115

Formal awareness, 48-51

Gagne, Robert, 2, 40

Garfield, Eugene, 109(43)

Gray, William S., 44(47)

Green, Samuel S., 38-39

Group counseling, 82-102

Group negotiation, 82-102